This book belongs to...

_____

a woman who desires
to live a better life.

Small Changes
for a Better
Life

Elizabeth George

HARVEST HOUSE PUBLISHERS

EUGENE, OREGON

Cover by Terry Dugan Design, Minneapolis, Minnesota

Cover photo © Dana Edmunds, Getty Images

Acknowledgment

As always, thank you to my dear husband, Jim George, M. Div., Th. M., for your able assistance, guidance, suggestions, and loving encouragement on this project.

SMALL CHANGES FOR A BETTER LIFE
(previously published as *God's Wisdom for a Woman's Life*)
Copyright © 2003 by Elizabeth George
Published by Harvest House Publishers Eugene, Oregon 97402
www.harvesthousepublishers.com

Library of Congress Cataloging-in-Publication Data

George, Elizabeth, 1944-
 [God's wisdom for a woman's life]
 Small changes for a better life/Elizabeth George.
   p.cm.
 ISBN-13: 978-0-7369-1729-2 (pbk.)
 ISBN-10: 0-7369-1729-2
 1. Christian women—Religious life. I. Title.
 BV4527.G4592 2006
 248.8'43—dc22   2005024828

Printed in the United States of America

06 07 08 09 10 11 12 13 14 /BP-KB/ 10 9 8 7 6 5 4 3 2

Contents

Seeking a
Better Life

I'm sure your life is complex and demanding...just like mine. You wear a multitude of hats, possess a long list of responsibilities, and are expected to live out your many roles. On top of these assignments, you're also supposed to be a time management expert, take care of your appearance, watch what you eat, maintain a high level of discipline, oversee your spiritual growth, follow through on all things with diligence...*and* practice your priorities! Are you thinking, "Help! I need a better life"?

What's a woman to do? In this life-changing book, you'll find out the how-to's and practicalities for mastering these everyday challenges. As you work your way through principles that never fail to improve a woman's life, you'll discover...

    ❧ ways to improve your life one day at a time,

    ❧ insights for setting new priorities,

    ❧ a blueprint for a better life,

    ❧ small changes that bring order to your life, and

❧ tools for building the life you desire.

This is just a sample of the wonders you'll encounter on the journey we will take in this book—a journey to gain practical, working knowledge. Along the way we'll also gather timeless principles from the Bible, for..."the LORD gives wisdom; from *His* mouth come knowledge and understanding" (Proverbs 2:6).

Also, don't miss out on the companion volume to this book, *Small Changes for a Better Life Growth and Study Guide*. Whether alone or in a group, you'll enjoy the additional principles and scriptures in this study guide that address the day-in, day-out areas of your busy life.

Dear seeker of a better life, there is help. And there is hope. Read on to discover how you can live out God's plan for you. Prepare yourself—you're about to discover your better life!

God's
Plan
for Your
Life

Wisdom is skill in living.[1]

Wisdom is the right use of knowledge.[2]

Wisdom is knowing what to do.

Wisdom is the ability to see with discernment.

Wisdom is the ability to view life as God perceives it.[3]

Wisdom is the God-given ability to see life with rare
objectivity and to handle life with rare stability.[4]

Ask for Wisdom

J don't know about you, but it seems like I have to make at least one decision a second. Sometimes I feel like life's demands are bombarding me on all fronts. And every assault calls for something from me—a word, an answer, a judgment call, an action, a choice. I have to decide what to think or not think, say or not say, ask or let lie, work on or wait on. I even have to determine whether to buy or not buy, pause or move into action, get up or sit down. In a word, what I need is *wisdom* for making the decisions that lead to a better life. Can you relate?

How do we get wisdom? How do we get on the path to living out God's plan for our lives? One man in the Bible—Solomon—shows us the Number One way: We must simply learn to ask God for help—for wisdom.

"Lord, Give Me Wisdom!"

Solomon was the son of the mighty King David and Israel's new king. In addition, he was somewhat young (1 Kings 3:7), had lived his whole life in his father's large shadow, and was definitely inexperienced. You can read his full story in

1 Kings 1:1–11:43. As he possibly quaked in his sandals and staggered under the weight of his new responsibility, Solomon did what you and I must learn to do if we desire a better life. He took the first step: He went to God in prayer and asked for wisdom. He basically prayed, "Lord, give me wisdom!"

I'm sure you are familiar with the "genie and lamp" scenario of "ask anything you wish and it will be granted." Well, this is essentially what happened to Solomon. In a dream the Lord appeared to Solomon and said, "Ask! What shall I give you?" (1 Kings 3:5).

What would you ask for?

Solomon shows us the right thing to ask for bettering your life. He answered, "Give to Your servant an understanding heart to judge Your people, that I may discern between good and evil. For who is able to judge this great people of Yours?" (verse 9).

And the result?

God was pleased with Solomon's request. Therefore He said to Solomon, "Because you have asked this thing, and have not asked long life for yourself, nor have asked riches for yourself, nor have asked the life of your enemies, but have asked for yourself understanding to discern justice, behold, I have done according to your words; see, I have given you a wise and understanding heart, so that there has not been anyone like you before you, nor shall any like you arise after you" (verses 11-12).

Then came the bonus!

"And I have also given you what you have not asked: both riches and honor, so that there shall not be anyone like you among the kings all your days" (verse 13).

And by the way, Solomon became the wisest man who ever lived (other than Jesus Christ, of course). He is heralded as a man who spoke 3,000 proverbs (1 Kings 4:32). In the book of Proverbs you can read the best of his 3,000 wise sayings. He was truly brilliant because God blessed him and "God gave Solomon wisdom and exceedingly great understanding" (1 Kings 4:29).

Daily Steps Toward a Better Life

Several daily steps will improve the quality of your life and move you toward discovering God's plan.

Step 1—Desire wisdom. Go a step further and desire wisdom *above all else*. This is the first giant step toward wisdom. Solomon desired wisdom, and he desired it above all the other things the human heart can desire.

Take the temperature of your heart's yearnings. Do you desire long life and riches (1 Kings 3:11), or do you desire wisdom? Check your heart. Solomon says, "Happy is the man [or woman] who finds wisdom, and the man who gains understanding; for her proceeds are better than the profits of silver, and her gain than fine gold" (Proverbs 3:13-14).

Step 2—Pray for wisdom. Again, that's what Solomon did. He recognized his need for wisdom…and acted on it by asking God for it. He didn't pray for a good marriage, or obedient children, or money to pay the bills, or a promotion at work. No, he prayed, "Give me wisdom and knowledge" (2 Chronicles 1:10).

When you pray for wisdom and knowledge, you are more likely to gain the wisdom required to have a better marriage and more obedient children, manage your time and money so the bills get paid, and exel at your work. Success is bound up in wisdom. What do you pray for? It's not wrong to pray for your job and finances, marriage and family. But be sure you are primarily praying for the *one* thing that will better *every* thing in your life. Check your prayers. Are you asking God for wisdom? One of my favorite scriptures regarding wisdom was written by Solomon in Proverbs 2: "Cry out for discernment, and lift up your voice for understanding" (verse 3). Echoing this wisdom about a thousand years later, the apostle James wrote, "If any of you lacks wisdom, let him ask of God...and it will be given to him" (James 1:5). So ask! Pray for wisdom. Your life will be better!

Step 3—Seek wisdom. Proverbs 2 continues, "If you seek her as silver, and search for her as for hidden treasures; then you will understand the fear of the LORD, and find the knowledge of God" (verses 4-5). When I first began studying Proverbs, I remember being impressed by the effort it takes a miner to excavate jewels, silver, and gold. It requires blood, sweat, and tears. Why? Because such treasure does not lie exposed to the casual passerby. No one on a little stroll through life will observe such riches by chance. No, they are buried. They are out of sight...sealed away, awaiting discovery. And only the diligent, the devoted, and the determined will put forth the strenuous labor required to find them. Next Solomon tells us point blank where to seek wisdom: "For the LORD gives wisdom; from His mouth come knowledge and understanding" (verse 6). Here is our biggest clue yet to finding the treasure of hard-won wisdom for a better life—it's in the Bible!

Do you diligently and strenuously seek the treasure of wisdom? Are you digging through the Bible? Do your personal goals include this assignment from God to seek wisdom? If so, your life will be bettered day by day as you search the Scriptures.

Step 4—Grow in wisdom. Solomon is a strong example of a person who desired wisdom, prayed for wisdom, and sought wisdom. But unfortunately he also provides us with a negative example of a person who failed in this vital fourth step to wisdom—he did not *grow* in wisdom. Early on Solomon desired a better life, recognized his need for wisdom, sought it, and stunned the nation with his keen wisdom (1 Kings 3:16-28). But then he took many foreign wives who led him into idolatry, and his desire for wisdom and his follow-through on God's timeless principles of wisdom waned. In the end Solomon failed to obey God, neglected to grow in wisdom, and silently slipped off the pages of Scripture. Little is recorded about the last decade of Solomon's reign over God's people. Sadly, to this day, he is known not only for the wisdom God gave him, but also as the man who had "700 wives and 300 concubines" (1 Kings 11:3). What an epitaph!

A Woman of Amazing Wisdom

Now I want you to meet a woman who shows us the beauty—and benefits—of wisdom. In contrast to King Solomon, she was not in a national leadership position and did not have a prestigious title. No, she was a wife and a home manager, a woman very much like you. But she was also a woman who possessed a great measure of wisdom—

wisdom that not only bettered her hard and bitter life, but saved it and the lives of many others.

Meet Abigail

Abigail (whose story is told in 1 Samuel 25:1-42) was a woman who had to make a decision a second too. Married to an alcoholic tyrant named Nabal (meaning "fool"), you can only imagine the tightrope she walked. Yet Abigail is applauded as a woman of wisdom, a woman whose life was characterized by sound, wise actions and speech. Her most amazing act of wisdom was averting a bloodbath between her foolish husband and the avenging warrior David and his 400 troops. Abigail knew when to act...and did. She knew what to do...and did it. And she knew what to say...and said it. What were some of the marks of Abigail's wisdom?

- She perceived the big picture.
- She kept her composure.
- She formed a plan.
- She spoke with wisdom.
- She effectively influenced others.

Abigail's life teaches us that every challenge or responsibility that lies before us can be handled in a better way when we handle it with God's wisdom.

Just for Today...

Do you desire a better life, one distinguished by greater wisdom? Then just for today make small changes and begin forming daily habits that will help you live God's plan for you.

❏ Just for today...read the chapter of the book of Proverbs that corresponds with the date of this month. Pick the one verse that most speaks to your heart and your life situation. Go a step further and write it on a 3" x 5" card. Carry it with you all day. Prop it up near the sink when you're at work in the kitchen. Lay it on the counter when you wash your face, brush your teeth, put on makeup, and fix your hair. Slip it into your purse to pull out and review when waiting at a stoplight. Have a goal to make the wisdom of that one proverb yours.

❏ Just for tomorrow...think about some decision you must make or some problem you are facing. Then heed the wisdom of Solomon and pray! Ask God for wisdom. Also put Proverbs 15:22 to work. It teaches us that "without counsel, plans go awry, but in the multitude of counselors they are established." Who will you ask for help?

❏ Just for this week...purchase or check out from your church library a commentary (a book of explanation written by a Bible scholar) on the book of Proverbs. (I've included a list of such books in the Bibliography at the back of this book.) Then each day as you read, follow along in the commentary. You'll be amazed by your growth. This is one simple way to better your life.

Living God's Plan

Throughout this book about small changes for a better life, we'll be looking at what the Bible says about God's plan for you and how to live it out. But you can begin right now by taking this one small, wise step: "The man who is truly wise is the man who finds out that he is a fool without Christ [Romans 1:22]....As long as a man rejects Christ, he is a fool. The wisest man is he who, in complete abandonment to self, bows before the Lord."[5]

Have you bowed yourself before the Lord? Your better life—indeed, *your best life!*—begins the second you do.

*G*od's *G*uidelines for a *B*etter *L*ife

❧ Make sure you treat each day as being important—*"Teach us to number our days, that we may gain a heart of wisdom"* (Psalm 90:12).

❧ Admit your need for wisdom...and ask for it—*"If any of you lacks wisdom, let him ask of God, who gives to all liberally and without reproach, and it will be given to him"* (James 1:5).

❧ Work at developing a deep respect for God—*"The fear of the LORD is the beginning of wisdom, and the knowledge of the Holy One is understanding"* (Proverbs 9:10).

❧ Be sure you have a vital relationship with Jesus Christ—*"I...do not cease to...[make] mention of you in my prayers: that the God of our Lord Jesus Christ, the Father of glory, may give to you the spirit of wisdom and revelation in the knowledge of Him"* (Ephesians 1:15-17).

❧ Be willing to pay any price for the truth—*"Buy the truth, and do not sell it, also wisdom and instruction and understanding"* (Proverbs 23:23).

"I am not all that I should be, but I am bringing all my energies to bear on this one thing: Forgetting the past and looking forward to what lies ahead, I strain to reach the end of the race and receive the prize for which God is calling us up to heaven because of what Christ Jesus did for us."
(PHILIPPIANS 3:13-14 TLB)

Put first things first and we get second things thrown in:
Put second things first and we lose both first and second things.[1]

The more you focus on God's priorities for you and practice those priorities, the more you will eventually live by them. Then you will be living out God's plan for you, a life of order.[2]

Order Your Life

One picture is worth a thousand words. And the picture painted in Proverbs 31:10-31 of a woman who knew all about living a better life has served me well through my busy days and years. This woman is the ultimate model of someone who lived out God's plan and priorities for her. Through her portrait, you and I can walk beside a loving and powerful mentor as seen in the span of her busy-but-orderly life. We can witness and watch the daily steps she took that made for a better life for her, for her family, and for her community.

To this day whenever I read the 22 verses that depict the details of her day-in, day-out life, I instantly gain three things—renewed strength for my efforts, a fresh reminder of God's priorities for my life, and a new dedication to His plan for my time here on earth. Visiting with this lady is such an energy charge that I've memorized these scriptures so I can carry her "Tips for a Better Life" with me in my heart. Then I can call upon God's counsel through her at any time, in any place, and in every situation.

The first time I read about this remarkable woman from the Bible, I marveled at her wisdom, her energy, her focus. Then I wondered, "How did she do it all? This woman seemed to be *everywhere* at all times, taking care of *everyone* and *everything*! What was her secret?"

The Proverbs 31 woman was no Wonder Woman or superhero. No, she was a busy woman just like you and me. But one of her distinctive marks was knowing and practicing her priorities. She knew God's plan for her and zeroed in on living it out. Many women don't have a clear understanding of their priorities. Therefore they rush off in all directions at once...or in no direction at all. Other women know their priorities but fail to live by them. They end up walking through life with guilt and frustration. But the wise woman understands her priorities and lives them—and enjoys a better life!

So what do we learn from this accomplished woman and from other teachings in the Bible about God's plan and our priorities? What clues can we find about the small changes we can make to instantly better our lives? And what does she show us about where we should be placing the emphasis of our time, energy, and efforts?

Priority One—Put God First

Top billing goes to God—*always*. Our love for God and our devotion to Him are to be complete and all-consuming. The woman in Proverbs 31 was praised by God and others as "a woman who fears the Lord" (verse 30). And, according to Proverbs 9:10, "The fear of the Lord" is the beginning of all wisdom and understanding. Jesus put it this way, "'You shall love the Lord your God with all your heart, with all your soul, with all your mind, and with all your strength.' This is the first commandment" (Mark 12:30).

The most important step to living a better life is to choose to put God first as the reigning priority of your life and of each fresh new day. That includes making one very practical decision every day—to read something out of God's Word. You see, God's plan for your life is revealed in His Word, the Bible. Therefore, spending some time each day in God's Word is a must for discovering His design for your life and your day.

And just to secure the place of this leading priority, I try to read the Bible early in the day. I purpose to do it first thing each day, to put first things first. My thinking goes like this: *I want God to be first in my life, so I'm putting Him first in my life today.* When you and I make—and act on—this one decision, we experience this truth: "Put first things first and we get second things thrown in; put second things first and we lose both first and second things."[3]

If you want a better life, then make this one small change. Before the day gets going (or gets out of control!) and before the others in your household get going, curl up in a cozy place and read your Bible. Fill your mind with God's mind. This one simple act of beginning your day with God brings order to your life and sets each day on the path toward living out God's plan.

Priority Two—Serve Others

After Jesus made the statement in Mark 12:30 regarding the love we are to have for God—a love that includes our obedience to Him—He said, "And the *second* [commandment],

like it, is this: 'You shall love your neighbor as yourself'"
(Mark 12:31).

God first, others second. This is the order of priorities
being lived out in the Proverbs 31 woman. The others in her
life were her husband, her children, her helpers and co-
workers, and those in her community. And these people
received the overflow of her first-love for the Lord. Each
day, after looking first to God and receiving from Him, this
noble woman next turned her eyes, hands, and heart toward
others. God's love was extended to the priority people
nearest to her. This lady's life was spent serving others.
That's why she was praised by God, by her husband and
children, and by the community. Why, even "her own
works," her very accomplishments, "praised" her (Proverbs
31:28-31)!

The following three steps will help you better order your
life as you live God's plan to serve others.

Know God's order of priorities—Thinking "God first and
others second" brings about a better life as it guides me in
planning each day. Understanding that I am to do all things
in Him and *through* Him and *for* Him and *unto* Him gives
my every day and every act of my every day an upward
focus. Each day I try to plan exactly how to bless and serve
my husband, my two daughters and their husbands and
seven children. My planning extends to include my friends
and neighbors, my church family, and the women I minister
to. "God first and others second" is a simple step toward
living out God's plan and order for our lives. So let the out-
pouring of service begin! This one change will better the
lives of others, including your own.

Plan to practice God's priorities—Take your planner or calendar in hand. Look at your plan for tomorrow. Does it include priority time with God? If not, take your pen and mark it indelibly on your schedule as the first thing. When I consider this Number One act, I never fail to hear the echo of Jesus' words in my heart—"Without Me you can do nothing" (John 15:5). Oh, how I need to remember that!

Next look to see if tomorrow's plan includes your loved ones. First, list them. Then ask, "What will I do for each one of them? And when?" Make the appropriate markings. Then fill up the rest of the day with the multitude of activities that make up the rich, wonderful, multifaceted days of your life. And speaking of rich—what a rich reward you will receive at the end of a day spent in this way! Oh, you'll be tired. Count on it! But welcome it too. You'll be fulfilled because you lived out God's plan for you for one entire day. You lived just one day according to God's top two priorities—God first and others second.

Eliminate nonessential activities—It's not only *God* before all others, but it's also other *people* before a multitude of *other things* we could spend our time on. These "other things" can keep us from serving people, whether it's our husband, children, and parents, or friends, neighbors, workmates, and people at church and in the community.

What kinds of other things? Things like laziness. Too much sleeping in. Napping. Lounging. Things like too much shopping and running around. Things like too much time spent on the telephone, on the Internet, watching TV, or working on hobbies...even things like too much time spent with friends or working at a job. It's easy to let attention to secondary and lesser things crowd out God's plan for us to take care of His first two priority areas of our lives—God first and others second.

Priority Three—Take Care of Yourself

Now for yourself. Yes, there is a place for taking care of yourself. There'll be more on this priority area in other sections, but I want to emphasize here and now that taking care of yourself improves your service to God and others.

For instance, take these all too common scenarios (maybe even from your life!). You fail to exercise...so your back goes out or you find yourself trying to function in a depressed, defeated, discouraged, lifeless state. You fail to watch what you eat...so you lack energy or develop high blood pressure. You fail to get your necessary sleep (there's the TV, Internet, and hobby time again!)...so you can't get up, get going, or get it together the next day. You fail to practice discipline in the pills you take or the caffeine you ingest...so you are unpredictable, unreliable, and unstable, causing the others in your life (and the quality of your life...your better life!) to suffer. You fail to take your vitamin supplements or prescribed medications and to drink enough water...so you lack the vitality and health needed in your daily life of service to God and others.

I'm sure you're getting the picture! There is a danger in neglecting your health and good habits. After all, where does the physical energy come from for living out God's priorities and roles for your life? It comes from taking care of yourself, which is a part of God's plan for you.

Please note, there is a distinction between selfishness and taking care of yourself. Selfishness is self-indulgence, self-serving, and self-focus, which hinders our service to God and others. Tending to yourself, however, enhances and strengthens your service to God and others. In other words, you are to take care of yourself so you can live out God's priorities. As with all of God's priorities, this one requires planning too.

So...get out your day planner again. You've already scheduled in #1—Time with God and #2—Time for serving others. Now plan in #3—Time for taking care of yourself. For instance, *when* will you get up and go to bed? *When* will you eat...and *what*? *When* will you exercise...and *what* exercises? And don't forget your vitamin supplements—*when* will you take them? Your planning and your planner will help you live out God's priority of taking care of yourself.

When it comes to yourself, follow God's formula—

- deny yourself of overindulgence (Proverbs 23:2 and 30:8),

- examine yourself for any sinful habits (1 Corinthians 11:28),

- exercise yourself to godliness (1 Timothy 4:7), and

- develop self-control (Galatians 5:23).

Just for Today...

How do you and I live out God's plan? How can we better our lives? The answer is a small-but-big one—by living God's way one day at a time. By practicing God's order for us one day at a time. So make the changes necessary to live out what you're learning about God's priorities for your life. Begin today...and extend them for a lifetime!

❏   Just for today...order and plan tomorrow according to the three priority areas of God, others, and self. Regarding time in God's Word, what book of the Bible would you like to read or learn more about? If you don't know where to start, begin with Proverbs 31:10-31. Regarding others, what will you specifically do to serve your husband, children, family members, friends, and the rest of the people in your daily life? And for yourself, what's wrong? What needs attention or correction? What's not what it should be and needs improvement? Take an honest, hard look. Then plan to make changes tomorrow—however small—for just one day. It will be a better day!

❏   Just for tomorrow...follow your priority plan. Stick to your guns. And be prepared—you'll have to say *no*...to yourself, to your flesh, to your excuses. But God will help you do it. All you have to do is make it through one day. To order your life, get up when you planned to. Read your Bible when you planned to. Do the acts of love you planned that will signal to others they are truly a priority. And take care of yourself. Wow, what a day that will be! And what a giant, commendable step toward living out God's plan for you! Tomorrow will be glorious!

❏   Just for this week...do what you planned each day. Multiply your one good day by seven. And keep a record of your progress. It's evidence of God's grace, and it's encouragement for you. Journal the results of your new disciplines. Notice and note the strength you are gaining as you read your Bible. Then enter your list of good deeds performed for the people in your life, which is more evidence of God's grace. The act of taking time to keep a record of your daily steps will help move you toward your better life and bring glory to God as you "remember" His goodness and the "marvelous works which He has done" (Psalm 105:5). You'll marvel as you see your small decisions developing you into a woman who knows and practices her priorities. Wow, what a week that will be! A week of order you'll want to repeat...for life. Hello...better life!

Living God's Plan

I hope you noticed the scripture at the beginning of this chapter, Philippians 3:13-14. Take another look at it. A loud message this passage shouts to every woman who wants to live out God's plan for her is this—the Christian life requires focus. And the constant exercise of living according to priorities ingrains it into your life. It makes all the difference in achieving a better life. The more you focus on God's priorities for you and practice those priorities, the more you will live by them. Then you will be living out God's plan for you—a life of order.

God's Guidelines for a Better Life

❧ Fix God first in your heart—*"Seek first the kingdom of God and His righteousness, and all these things shall be added to you"* (Matthew 6:33).

❧ Take care of the people at home—*"She also rises while it is yet night, and provides food for her household, and a portion for her maidservants"* (Proverbs 31:15).

❧ Contribute to those in your community—*She extends her hand to the poor, yes, she reaches out her hands to the needy"* (Proverbs 31:20).

❧ Keep moving!—*"She...does not eat the bread of idleness"* (Proverbs 31:27).

❧ Remember, the Lord is the reason for all that you do—*"A woman who fears the LORD, she shall be praised"* (Proverbs 31:30).

God has purposes for our lives which He has
not yet revealed. Therefore each day grows
sacred in wondering expectation.

—Phillips Brooks

"Teach us to number our days, that we may gain
a heart of wisdom."

(Psalm 90:12)

Each day, with the gift of a whole, entire, precious, and
priceless day before you, ask: "Lord, how do You want me
to live this day? What is it You want me to do with this
one day You have given me? What is the work You
want me to accomplish today?"

—Elizabeth George

Own Your Purpose

I love interacting with women almost every day through letters, the Internet, radio phone-ins, or in live question-and-answer sessions. I so enjoy getting to know their hearts as they seek help for bettering the different areas of their challenging lives. I hear things like "Help...I have four little ones!" "Help...I have grandchildren on one end of my busy life and ailing parents on the other!" "Help...my husband is trying so hard to provide for the family that I feel like I never see him!" (I also have my own personal set of "Help..." pleas!)

But what I mostly hear is that like me, busy women tend to bog down in the day-to-day matters of life. We lose sight of how the work we are doing today fits into God's purpose and plan for our lives and our futures. We forget to look upward, forward, and beyond the moment due to today's sense of urgency.

Yet these are the looks that clarify the purpose for what we're doing, need to be doing, or are struggling to do. When we fail to look to God for His vision and help, we settle into a life of muddling through each day, barely making it to its unglorious end, failing to comprehend its purpose and where it fits in the grand scheme of our lives. Sadly, most women are merely eking out the hours of their day. Some, too, are muttering their way through their day, frustrated, hopeless, even bitter.

But here's a truth that sheds new light on each one-day span—you and I have no guarantee on the length of our lives. No, all we have is our one day—today. Therefore we must seek to live each one-day time allotment with the future and a purpose in mind. An understanding of God's purposes and a long-range view of life changes and betters our every day and its endeavors...thus bettering our lives!

One small step that will better your life is to form the habit of regularly asking these important questions about your life and evaluating your answers:

- What is God's plan and purpose for my life?

- In the end, what do I want to have accomplished with my life?

- And how do I want my life to have contributed to others?

- What do I want to leave behind?

Look now at some of the more important facets of a woman's life, facets that reveal the *whys* of life and its purpose. Keep in mind as you read that *purpose* is the object for which something exists or is done. For us that "object" is God. *Purpose* is also the end in view, our future. Again, for us, that is God. I'll use words such as *purpose, purposes,* and *future* interchangeably because not only is our purpose wrapped up in God, but our future is too.

Enjoy the Promise of Eternal Life

Our time on earth definitely has its joys. But it also has its trials and sorrows. But no matter how hard or tiring our work on earth becomes, it is invigorating when we realize that at life's end, we will enjoy the presence of the Lord forever. We will enjoy the *best* life forever! The anticipation of eternal life adds hope to each and every day and deed. If you're anything like me, you can endure almost anything if you know some reward is coming. And one reason why you and I can stand anything that comes our way is because of what we're able to look forward to—the magnificent inheritance of eternal life with God, which is reserved in heaven for those who believe (1 Peter 1:3-5). We are also assured that in God's presence there is "fullness of joy," and at His right hand await "pleasures forevermore" (Psalm 16:11).

Do you possess the hope of eternal life, my friend? It's the best *why* of life! And it is a gift of God given to us through faith in His Son, Jesus Christ (John 1:12). If you do have this hope, you can live each and every day, no matter how difficult or dreary, in the sunshine of God's promise of eternal life. If you don't have this hope, why don't you pray the following prayer now?

> Jesus, I know I am a sinner, and I want to repent of my sins and turn and follow You. I believe that You died for my sins and rose again victorious over the power of sin and death, and I want to accept You as my personal Lord and Savior. Come into my life, Lord Jesus, and help me follow and obey You from this day forward. Help me grow in You. Amen.

If you just prayed this prayer, contact a Christian you know or a pastor of a church and tell him or her about your desire to know Christ. Start attending a Bible teaching church and reading your Bible. You've just stepped into a better life—one centered in Jesus!

Grow in Your Spiritual Life

Next is your spiritual life. We were created by God and for God. Therefore we should be growing in the Lord each day. This ensures us of a better life and helps accomplish several more of God's purposes for us—that we be conformed into the image of His Son (Romans 8:29) and that we renew our minds (Romans 12:2) and our inner lives day by day (2 Corinthians 4:16).

Why grow? Because God expects us to grow spiritually. A group of Christians in the Bible who failed to grow was chastised with these words: "By this time you ought to be teachers, [but] you need someone to teach you" (Hebrews 5:12). Growth is one of God's goals for your life. Therefore it instantly becomes one of your purposes.

And here's another reason—energy! (And we both know that more energy equals a better life!) One of the bright rewards of spiritual growth is the tremendous energy it brings to each day and each task. As you read the Bible, the supernatural power of the Word of God energizes every daily task. It brings God's perspective on your life and on your work...to each day and its duties. That divine perspective then infuses you and your work with stamina, drive, purpose, enthusiasm...and energy! It's a case of God's purposes empowering and pushing and encouraging you to do what you have to do, what you must do.

Get a Handle on Your Practical Life

God's purposes are also revealed in the practical areas of life. For instance, what is your practical life made up of? Many women's lists look something like this:

Family life—Everyone has family: parents, siblings, and extended kin. And if you are married, your daily life includes a husband...and in-laws. If you have children, add them to your life list. The people God has placed in your life become part of His purposes for your life. He means for you to invest your time, effort, energy, and money into your family. He even speaks in the Bible to your specific roles in each relationship. (More on this in chapters to come.) Therefore, doing what God says He wants you to do in these family relationships becomes a life purpose. If the only thing you ever leave behind is a godly imprint upon your family, then you will have lived out one of God's grandest purposes.

Physical life and health—Where does the physical energy come from for living out God's purposes and plans? From your body. And God has entrusted you with the stewardship of your body.

You know from experience that any neglect in your physical live and health ultimately brings consequences. Yet it's human nature to erroneously think that you have all the time in the world to fulfill God's purpose for yourself in this area. You know you're *going* to get around to it. You have great plans to change your eating habits, to exercise more, to take better care of yourself, to be more regular in taking your vitamin supplements, to reduce stress, to alter your lifestyle, to give up your bad habits...one of these days. And the whole time you're meaning to do something and intending to change, bad habits and neglect are taking their toll...until one day your health is worse than you thought, jeopardizing your future.

How's your physical condition and your health? You can be sure that what you're doing or neglecting to do in the care of your health now will determine your quality of life in the future. It's the biblical principle of sowing and reaping: "For whatever a man sows, that he will also reap" (Galatians 6:7). Now, what will that quality be?

Ministry life—Every day I ask myself the questions I shared earlier: "In the end, what do I want to have accomplished with my life? And how do I want my life to have contributed to others? What do I want to leave behind?" These are sobering questions about life, aren't they? Obviously loving and caring for my family members is an urgent priority and one of God's primary purposes for me. I am to contribute to their lives positively and for Christ. But beyond them, in the end...how many lives will I have touched? People are one of God's purposes, for in the end, all God will redeem from this planet are the souls of people. So beyond your family members, how many women and children are you mentoring, training, and teaching? How many others are you serving, helping, giving to, and talking to about Jesus Christ?

Manage Your Daily Life

It's true that our days are numbered. Indeed, they are in God's hands. He and He alone knows the length of our days on earth. In reality, then, that makes the minutes of a day all we have. That means, as two age-old sayings go, "Today is all you have" and "There is no tomorrow." Jesus taught these truths in His parable of the rich fool who tore down his barns to build bigger ones. What did God say to this man? "Fool! This night your soul will be required of you" (Luke 12:20).

No, the on-purpose woman knows not to say or think or act as if "today or tomorrow we will go to such and such a city" or do such and such a thing. Why? Because she knows the rest of the story: "You do not know what will happen tomorrow. For what is your life? It is even a vapor that appears for a little time and then vanishes away." She knows to say and think instead, "If the Lord wills, we shall live and do this or that" (James 4:13-15). She knows that today is all she has and there is no tomorrow.

Dear friend, each 24-hour portion that God chooses to give to you is to be lived *in* Him, *unto* Him, *for* Him, *by* His strength, and with *His* plans in mind. Why? Because today *is* the future. Today is all you have to live out God's purposes. There is no guarantee of tomorrow.

But good news! The best thing about the future is that it comes only one day at a time. Today is all you have…but you do have today! That means today is the only future you have. Today is the only day you have to live out God's purposes. How you manage today adds to the quality of the better life—and future—you are building. And hopefully, you are building your life and future purposefully and with God's glory in mind.

Each day when I wake up, I can hardly believe how blessed I am. Just think, the gift of a day—a whole, entire, precious, and priceless day! But (I remind myself)—it's not *my* day. Oh no. It's *God's* day! And I am a steward of it. So I sit down with my calendar and planner in hand and ask, "Lord, how do You want me to live this day? What is it that You want me to do with this one day that You have given me? What is the work You want me to accomplish today?"

This is how God's purposes are lived out in the present. Not a day is to be taken for granted. Not a day is to be wasted or frittered away. And every day is meant to count. What is it that makes a day count, and makes it count for a better life? Answer: Living it for God's purposes. So make it your purpose to focus on...

- a godly walk—"And what does the Lord require of you but to do justly, to love mercy, and to walk humbly with your God" (Micah 6:8).

- a passionate walk—The apostle Paul declared, *"Reaching* forward to those things which are ahead, I *press* toward the goal for the prize of the upward call of God in Christ Jesus" (Philippians 3:13-14). Catch the passion of such a purpose!

- a sober walk—Warning! God cries, "See then that you walk circumspectly, not as fools but as wise, redeeming the time, because the days are evil" (Ephesians 5:15-16).

- a wise walk—"Therefore do not be unwise, but understand what the will of the Lord is" (Ephesians 5:17). Make it your purpose to know and understand what God's will is as revealed through His Word.

Just for Today...

Knowing your purpose is a powerful motivating force. Make it a habit to each day to reaffirm God's purposes for you and plan to live them out...just for today.

❏ Just for today…set your sights on God's plans and purposes for your life. Pray with calendar and planner in hand and ask, "Lord, how do You want me to live this day? What is it that You want me to do with this one day You have given me? What is the work You want me to accomplish today?" Then live out those purposes in a passionate and sober-minded way. Focus on "Him and them," on God and the people He's entrusted to you and given to you to serve. This will be one better day…contributing to your better life.

❏ Just for tomorrow…(if there is one!) welcome the gift of your new day—a whole, entire, precious, and priceless day! Then remember that it's not your day. No, it's God's day…and you are a steward of it. So take calendar and planner in hand and follow the path you've chosen above.

❏ Just for this week…watch over your walk with God, watch over your family and loved ones, and watch over yourself. Focus on these purposes for a better life.

Living God's Plan

Maybe you noticed this chapter is more philosophical than the others. But I put the subject of purpose here at the beginning of this book about a better life for a reason. I know too many women (and I used to be one of them!) who cannot sustain the pace of a forward-moving life. These sweet women know God's plan and His principles for a better life, and they want to apply them. But they have difficulty keeping up with their good intentions.

Why would that be? For many it's because they see no purpose in their days. Therefore there's no reason to strive. There's no *why* for what they are doing or trying to do. My new friend, *purpose is the key to doing what we have to do to live out God's plan for us.*

And what is God asking of us? What are His purposes? Beloved, God does not ask His women to do a thousand things, not even a hundred things. No, our all-wise God asks only a few things of us. In fact, I think what we've looked at here regarding God's purposes for us could be boiled down to just three:

❧ *Determine to obey God* (1 Samuel 15:22).

❧ *Develop a greater trust in the Lord* (Proverbs 3:4-6).

❧ *Devote your life to becoming more like Christ* (Romans 8:29).

As you are faithful in these three areas, you will find and fulfill God's purpose in your life. Any person—man or woman—who seeks to do these things will most definitely live a better life, a life of purpose (Ephesians 1:11; 2 Timothy 1:9).

*G*od's *G*uidelines for a *B*etter *L*ife

❧ Look not on what you have done, but on what Jesus has done—*"Not that I have already attained, or am already perfected; but I press on, that I may lay hold of that for which Christ Jesus has also laid hold of me"* (Philippians 3:12).

❧ Look to God, not yourself, for direction—*"Trust in the LORD with all your heart, and lean not on your own understanding; in all your ways acknowledge Him, and He shall direct your paths"* (Proverbs 3:5-6).

❧ Look at life with its briefness in mind—*"LORD, make me to know my end, and what is the measure of my days, that I may know how frail I am"* (Psalm 39:4).

❧ Look at what is straight in front of you— *"Wisdom is in the sight of him who has understanding, but the eyes of a fool are on the ends of the earth"* (Proverbs 17:24).

❧ Look to the finish line, not at the runners around you—*"Do you not know that those who run in a race all run, but one receives the prize? Run in such a way that you may obtain it"* (1 Corinthians 9:24).

God's
Plan
for Your
Spiritual
Life

For the Lord gives wisdom; from His mouth come
knowledge and understanding.
—Proverbs 2:6

God's Word is so exciting, so electric, so energizing—
in a word...thrilling. But more than that, God's Word is
life-changing. Its supernatural power is transforming,
and it provides direction for your life. For every need
and issue and decision that must be made in a
lifetime, the Bible has the answers.
—Elizabeth George

Read Your Bible

I don't know how passionately you feel about your Bible, but I can tell you that I consider my Bible to be my life. For my first 28 years on this earth I looked in every direction (but up!) for help. I read the world's wisdom about how to have a better life and a better marriage. The same went for child-raising. It's no wonder that on both counts things moved steadily from bad to worse. And my soul? I frantically sought peace in almost every place and religion you can think of.

And then I was put in a situation where I was required to read a "religious" book for a book review. The particular book I chose to review (because it was the one and only religious book in our house) quoted the Bible—*lots* of Bible. I mean verse after verse of Bible! Soon I began suspiciously thinking, "The Bible doesn't say that!"

At last I located my small, white, childhood confirmation Bible, dusted it off, and began to look up the Bible references. I was certainly unskilled at this (and maybe you can identify). For instance, if the reference was Daniel 4:7, I turned to the table of contents in my musty-smelling Bible, looked up the page number to the book of Daniel, then found the page and chapter, and finally the verse.

And there they were! The scriptures quoted by the writer of my one and only religious book were right there in the Bible. And as you and I both know, God's Word is powerful and mighty. It went to work on my hapless heart and sinking soul. Before I finished reading that book, I became, by God's grace, a Christian! I gave my life to Jesus Christ—every part and parcel of it. I was born again in Him and by Him and because of Him and unto Him. I entered into His forever family, and thanks be to Him, my life has never been the same. You see, I entered into the better—and the best!—life, life in Christ.

Since that day—the day I found out the truth about Jesus Christ in the Bible—I've been a helpless Bible addict. Even these decades later I still can't take in enough of God's Word. In fact, my appetite for the life-giving, life-saving, life-sustaining, problem-solving truths in God's Word has increased as the years have paraded by. I have now passed through what are called...

The Three Stages of Bible Reading

Stage 1—The cod liver oil stage when you take it like medicine.

Stage 2—The shredded wheat stage when it's nourishing but dry.

Stage 3—The peaches-and-cream stage when it is consumed with passion and pleasure.[1]

And now for you, my reading friend. I want you to have this same delicious addiction, love, and passion for God's Word. I want it for you because God's Word is so exciting, so electric, so energizing—in a word...thrilling. But more than that, I want it for you because God's Word, your Bible, is life-changing. Its supernatural power is transforming. And it provides direction for your life. Do you really want a better life? Then read your Bible. For every need and issue and decision that must be made in a lifetime, the Bible has the answers.

The Treasure of God's Word

At the beginning of this chapter is a verse from the book of Proverbs—"For the LORD gives wisdom; from His mouth come knowledge and understanding" (Proverbs 2:6). Solomon, the writer of Proverbs 2, cries out to you and me to *"seek"* wisdom and knowledge and understanding "as silver, and *search* for her as for hidden treasures" (verse 4). Truly, the Word of God is treasure. Why?

The Bible comes from God—The Bible is "given by inspiration of God" (2 Timothy 3:16), every word of it. That means it is "God-breathed." There are no fads and no gimmicks in the Bible. What you read between the covers of your Bible is wisdom for a lifetime, rock-solid, forever truth—truth you can stand on, live by, and trust...forever. Truth that brings about a better life.

I've already tried to express what the Bible, God's Word, means to me. Up until the day I dusted off that tiny Bible that had been given to a tiny girl (me!), I was lost in the pursuit of "the things in the world" (1 John 2:15). I read worldly books and listened to worldly voices. It was a baffling and frustrating life. Just when I was switching over my lifestyle to some particular view, along came another philosophy…and I had to start all over again! I had nothing to sink my teeth into, stand on, count on, or base my life on…until I found the Word of God. By contrast, God's truth will never change. Never! In the Bible you and I have God's grand plan for us. And we have His guidelines for our every need, for every issue, for every day, and forever.

That's my story. Now what's yours? Where are you on the Floundering Scale? On the Seeking Scale? On the Bible Appreciation Scale? If you're struggling or drifting along in life, I urge you to pick up a Bible and read. If you need help with a relationship, with a problem, with a decision you must make, then set up a personal retreat so you can spend time reading God's Word and praying. If you need a renewed passion for God's Word, then set aside some time each day dedicated to reading a portion of the Bible, even a small one. Immerse yourself in God's Word. And pray as you read. Commit yourself afresh to your spiritual growth, to your inner beauty, to the practice of reading your Bible. God's Word will make all the difference in the world…in every area of your life.

The Bible causes you to grow in Christlikeness—A beautiful picture of the transforming power of God's Word is written in 2 Corinthians 3:18: "But we all, with unveiled face, beholding as in a mirror the glory of the Lord, are being transformed into the same image from glory to glory, just as by the Spirit of the Lord." With these words the apostle Paul pointed out that all believers, as they continually focus on Christ, are transformed more and more into His image by the Holy Spirit.

You'll never hear me say I am Christlike, but you will always hear me say I desire to be Christlike. As I read my Bible and pray, I learn more about the life God intends me to live, the better life He's designed for His children. How about you? The simple exercise of reading your Bible is so rewarding and life-changing you'll want to do it for life...which will add up to a lifetime of growing spiritually, maturing in Christ, developing in the beauty of Christlikeness, and increasing in the knowledge of God's plan for you. In short, a better life.

And now, I ask you, what more do you and I need to convince us to be growing spiritually, to be gaining a better understanding of God's plan, to move toward a better life in Him? God calls us to ever seek knowledge and truth from Him, from His Word. Therefore, like those who mine for silver and search for gold, we who desire a better life must *search* the Scriptures daily, diligently, doggedly, devotedly, and desperately (Acts 17:11). Our lives depend on it! As we mine the spiritual wealth of wisdom in the Bible, we then possess the treasure of the message of God to our hearts, a message that changes our hearts and transforms us into the likeness of our blessed Savior.

Beloved, my heart is brimming over at this very moment! I have three Bibles open on my writing desk right this second (with four more on the shelf to my left, and I don't know how many—20? 30? 50?—more Bibles in Jim's library downstairs). And I'm going to take a break right now, grab my personal Bible, retreat to my easy chair, and pore over its pages yet again. The exercise of writing about the treasure of God's Word, reaching for the words to express its glory, and recalling the many wonderful changes it has effected in my life has created an urge I simply must respond to. I must go there now!

Unearthing the Treasure of God's Wisdom

(I'm back now.) Just how does our affection for God's Word grow? How does a book made up of ink on paper and bound between two covers translate into a passion, a passion that moves us to put out the effort required to gain the treasure? A few simple steps make it happen.

Step 1—Read it. I could add, *just* read it! Start anywhere. The only wrong way to read the Bible is not to read it. And don't make your Bible-reading time an ordeal. Just get your cup of coffee, tea, or hot chocolate, sit down, open your Bible, and read. Or take it to the doctor's office, or the hair salon, or the beach, or park, or on an airplane. Like a cup of nourishment, sip away on God's Word any and every place you are.

And while you're searching for God's plan for you as His child, read from the book of Proverbs. Expose yourself to God's wisdom every day by reading the chapter of Proverbs that corresponds with the date of the month. (And don't worry—it only takes about two minutes.) As I'm writing this sentence, it's November 24, which means I've revisited Proverbs 24 and its firm instruction about laziness (verses 30-34). (For some reason I always need that reminder!)

Whenever I hear women share about a mistake or a bad decision they've made, I always wonder in my heart, *Dear sweet woman, haven't you read the book of Proverbs? If you had ever read the book of Proverbs, even once, you would know exactly what God says to do and not to do about that issue*. As I said, just read it!

Step 2—Study it. There are many methods and levels of Bible reading. But I can promise you that if you begin to read your Bible, it won't be long before you have a few questions. And that will lead you to studying the Bible.

That's precisely what happened to me as I began to read from Proverbs every day. Soon I was wondering, "What in the world does *that* mean?" The same thing happened when I read about the women of the Bible. Growing up without Christian models, I turned to the women of the Bible for help. And soon the questions began to arrive.

So I purchased my first commentary about Proverbs. (See the Bibliography for a few titles.) Then I sought out a book that specialized in the lives of the women of the Bible. And soon I was building a library, one that now contains workbooks, study guides, and Bible studies on different books of the Bible. Begin small, but do study your Bible.

Step 3—Hear it. We should never study God's Word in a vacuum. We need those who are gifted with knowledge and teaching ability to help us open the eyes and ears of our understanding. So be sure you regularly hear the Word of God expounded and explained (Hebrews 10:25).

Step 4—Memorize it. So many women tell me they can't memorize Scripture. Yet my three-year-old grandson Jacob is somehow able to memorize Bible verses. I can't help but think if a toddler can, you can too! You see, we don't always have a Bible in our hand, but we can have the Bible hidden in our hearts. Just make the commitment…and do it.

Step 5—Devour it. David described God's Word as "sweeter...than honey and the honeycomb" (Psalm 19:10). Jeremiah testified, "Your words were found, and I ate them, and Your word was to me the joy and rejoicing of my heart" (Jeremiah 15:16). Job declared, "I have treasured the words of His mouth more than my necessary food" (Job 23:12). As you devour God's Word, you'll "taste" His refreshment too.

Just for Today...

How often do you eat? Daily! How often should you seek the Lord's wisdom and plan for your better life through His Word? Daily! Every discipline we are developing through this book is being tended to...one day at a time. That's how we take daily steps toward living out God's plan for us. So...

❑   Just for today...read your Bible. Doing so will stir your soul, encourage your heart, and fuel your faith. Don't miss out on God's wisdom today. And when you discover it, note it in your journal. Record the wisdom you find for living a better life. If you're not sure where to begin, begin with the chapter of Proverbs that corresponds with the date of the month. And here's a statistic—"By spending 10 minutes a day, you can read through the whole Bible in a year."[2] Couldn't you read 10 minutes... just for today? It's a small thing that will definitely make for a better life. It's guaranteed!

❑   Just for tomorrow...continue what you began above, but add Matthew, chapter 1. If you read one chapter in the Gospels (Matthew, Mark, Luke, and

John) every day, you will read through the life of Christ once every three months. That's four times a year. Multiply that by the remaining number of years in your life, and...well, you will have a treasure-house filled with the knowledge of your Savior's life. Then whatever comes your way, you can, by His grace, follow in His steps (1 Peter 2:21).

❏ Just for this week...think about another fact: Only about five percent of all Christians read through the Bible even once in their lives. By the time this week is over, you will be 1/52nd of the way toward joining the ranks of the elite "Top Five Percent." If you're faithful just for this week, you'll be well on your way to forging a habit that will reap eternal benefits and a better life here on earth. Peter put it this way: "All flesh is as grass, and all the glory of man as the flower of the grass. The grass withers, and its flower falls away, but the word of the LORD endures forever" (1 Peter 1:24-25). Be wise! Invest your time in something that lasts forever.

Living God's Plan

Wow! Just think! It's all yours—God's inspired Word. And it causes you to grow in Christlikeness. And how does this powerful transformation take place? It's an inside job. *The Bible changes your heart.* God's Word is alive and powerful, and it works on what's inside, on the heart (Hebrews 4:12). As you read the Bible, you learn God's truth, identify wrong behavior, mend your ways, and receive positive training in righteousness (2 Timothy 3:16). God's Word works you over from the inside out. It gives you a complete spiritual makeover and performs open heart surgery at the same time. God's Word is the ultimate beauty treatment for every woman, including you.

This is certainly true for me. When I take just a few minutes daily to read my Bible, it penetrates my heart. It lifts my soul. It causes me to desire what God desires, to think more like God thinks, and to pursue what God wants me to pursue. It changes my perspective on the people, events, and circumstances of my day. And it makes for a better life. When my reading time is over, I find my mind at rest, my heart at peace, my head clear, and my direction and purpose for my day established. Obviously all of these changes that occur as a result of God's Spirit working through His Word make for a better life. May the same be true for you, dear heart-sister!

*G*od's *G*uidelines for a *B*etter *L*ife

❦ The Bible keeps you from sin—*"Your word I have hidden in my heart, that I might not sin against You"* (Psalm 119:11).

❦ The Bible leads you in the right direction—*"Your word is a lamp to my feet and a light to my path"* (Psalm 119:105).

❦ The Bible answers your questions—*"All Scripture is given by inspiration of God, and is profitable for doctrine, for reproof, for correction, for instruction in righteousness"* (2 Timothy 3:16).

❦ The Bible gives you discernment—*"For the word of God is living and powerful, and sharper than any two-edged sword, piercing even to the division of soul and spirit...and is a discerner of the thoughts and intents of the heart"* (Hebrews 4:12).

❦ The Bible is your ultimate treasure—*"The statutes of the LORD are right, rejoicing the heart. ...More to be desired are they than gold...sweeter also than honey and the honeycomb"* (Psalm 19:8,10).

Prayer does not fit us for the greater works; prayer is the greater work. Prayer is the miracle of redemption at work in us which will produce the miracle of redemption in the lives of others.

—Oswald Chambers

Study may make a biblical scholar; but prayer puts the heart under heavenly teaching and forms the wise and spiritual Christian.[1]

—Charles Bridges

Develop Your Prayer Life

*I*s that your cell phone ringing?" We hear this every day, don't we? The technological era has certainly arrived in a big way in recent years. I remember getting my first cell phone. It seemed like it cost a fortune, and it was almost the size of my purse. Besides that, the air time was very expensive! So expensive, in fact, that to keep from receiving calls or being tempted to make a call, I would leave my precious cell phone off. Needless to say, that first cell phone wasn't much use.

My current cell phone is far more useful—it's less expensive and more portable, so I'm not as hesitant to leave it on. In many ways my prayer life is like my current cell phone— I can pray anytime I want, anywhere I want, to anyone (God!) I want, for as long as I want.

But unlike my cell phone, there are no fees or roaming charges when talking to God. I don't have to go to the time and trouble to scroll through my directory, select, and then dial a number. I don't even need to purchase any paraphernalia to enable me to talk "hands free" while I'm in the car. No, I have a direct channel to the God of the universe

24/7—24 hours a day, 7 days a week, to the Maker of heaven and earth. How's that for technology? *Divine* technology!

Talk to God

With prayer being so easy, you'd think that we would pray a lot more than we do. After all, it's one of God's steps toward a better life. But prayer, like any other spiritual discipline, is just that—a discipline. And our "natural man"—our flesh and its sinful nature—resists any and all spiritual disciplines. So you and I must make some changes, beginning with making an effort to pray. Here are a few steps to help develop your prayer life, which is a part of God's plan for you as His child.

Step 1: Do it!—I could add, "Just do it!" Prayer, like any other habit, has to have a starting point. Why? Because you learn to pray by praying. Prayer is no different than learning how to cook, clean, care for a baby, type, paint, sew, use a computer, or the thousand other things you must do or are interested in doing. Experience is the best teacher.

Step 2: Do it badly—If you are a beginner at prayer—or perhaps getting started again—when you first start praying, you may think you're doing it badly. You may stumble and agonize over your words and concerns. But no prayer is ever done badly in God's eyes if your heart is right. Have you ever had one of your young children try to communicate with you? You appreciate his effort. You eagerly listen through the fidgeting and to the stuttering and jabbering as he searches for words in his limited vocabulary. You hang on every sound so you can decipher his words and encourage him as he tries. You don't want to miss a thing!

Well, the good news is your heavenly Father is like you...and even more so because of His perfection. He is perfectly kind, perfectly patient, and He loves it when you and I talk to Him, when we come to Him with our prayers, no matter how unpolished or simple.

Step 3: Do it regularly—When I was in junior high school, I played the violin. I didn't exactly excel at it, even with practice. But for sure, you didn't want to hear me when I didn't practice! Prayer is like that. Prayer, like anything else done faithfully and regularly, in time becomes more natural and normal. But when we are irregular at prayer, we feel awkward and don't quite know what to say to God. God doesn't expect you to wait until you can word your prayers flawlessly. He just wants to hear from you. Make the changes necessary to form the habit of checking in with God on a regular basis—preferably daily!

That's what David, "the sweet psalmist of Israel" (2 Samuel 23:1), did. He declared to God, "My voice You shall hear *in the morning*, O Lord; in the morning I will direct it to You, and I will look up" (Psalm 5:3). Another psalmist exulted, "*Seven times a day* I praise You" (Psalm 119:164), indicating that he prayed and praised numerous times because of a continual attitude of praise. When you fail to pray, you are in a sense saying you don't need God. And here's another thought—when you fail to pray, you are also saying that you're probably not even thinking about God! How can I say that? Because any and every thought about God moves our hearts to pray.

Step 4: Do it faithfully—Faithfulness is a mark of maturity. Faithful people can be trusted in what they say and do. And faithfulness is a necessary element in any relationship, especially in a relationship with God. We know God is faithful. He is unchanging and unchangeable. Faithfulness is one of His attributes (James 1:17). So to keep up your part of a relationship with God, you need to be faithful to God. And the best way to be faithful is through a constant prayer life.

And here's a side benefit to praying faithfully. Prayer helps you keep a clean slate with God. The Bible says if you and I are faithful to "confess our sins, He is faithful and just to forgive us our sins and to cleanse us from all unrighteousness" (1 John 1:9). Pray faithfully—it will keep you more faithful in your walk with God.

Step 5: Do it for life—The breathing in of air sustains life. It's a basic fact—as long as we breathe, we live. Therefore no sane person would ever decide, "I think I'll take some time off from breathing." No, breathing is necessary for life. And you must see prayer in the same way. Prayer is necessary for the Christian life, as well as for a better life. Just as you will breathe for as long as you live, you must also pray for as long as you live. Do it for life!

Follow Jesus' Model Prayer

Jesus gave His disciples a model prayer to follow, one from which we can learn numerous prayer principles. He didn't just say (as I've been doing), *Do it! Do it badly, Do it regularly, Do it faithfully,* and *Do it for life.* No, the Master Teacher gave His disciples a guide to follow. What is popularly called "The Lord's Prayer" has become a perfect pattern for prayer. A closer look at this model prayer gives us a better understanding of how to pray. Jesus, simply and straightforwardly, left no room for guesswork. He said to His followers, "When you pray, *say...*" (Luke 11:2), and...

> In this manner, therefore, pray: Our Father in heaven, hallowed be Your name. Your kingdom come. Your will be done on earth as it is in heaven. Give us this day our daily bread. And forgive us our debts, as we forgive our debtors. And do not lead us into temptation, but deliver us from the evil one. For Yours is the kingdom and the power and the glory forever. Amen (Matthew 6:9-13).

Prayer is personal. If you are one of God's children, you can talk to Him just like you talk to your physical father. And just as you would respect your earthly father, you are to be respectful of your Father in heaven. He is not "the Big Guy upstairs," "the Force," or "Mother Nature." Christ's model prayer begins with the very personal—and respectful—phrase, "Our Father in heaven" (verse 9).

Prayer acknowledges God's authority. The phrase "your kingdom come" (verse 10) recognizes God's rule. His physical kingdom is now in heaven but will soon be here on earth. That means you are a kingdom child waiting for the kingdom—and the King of kings!—to arrive.

Prayer acknowledges your trust. As a Christian, you do not accept such beliefs as fate, coincidence, luck, chance, or karma. That's because nothing in your life happens by accident. And nothing ever will. When you pray, "Your will be done" (verse 10), you are saying you trust a sovereign God to fulfill His perfect plan for your life.

Prayer indicates your dependence. You acknowledge that God is your sustainer and provider when you pray, "Give us this day our daily bread" (verse 11). You must never forget that God supplies your needs—every one of them. Whether you realize it or not, you are absolutely dependent on Him...even for the very bread you put in your mouth each day.

Prayer entreats God's guidance. "Life is a jungle!" is an often quoted description of our existence on this earth. It's easy to get lost in a jungle...but not if you have a guide. Your omnipresent, ever-present Guide watches out for you: "Do not lead us into temptation, but deliver us from the evil one" (verse 13). On the positive side, God guides you "in the paths of righteousness" (Psalm 23:3).

Just for Today...

What changes can you make to enjoy a better life? One is to pray just one day at a time. Prayer must be practiced today and every day for a lifetime. Martin Luther, the father of the Protestant Reformation, called prayer "the most important thing in my life." He admitted, "If I should neglect prayer for a single day, I should lose a great deal of the fire of faith." And the same is true for you if you are to live out God's plan in the midst of your complex, complicated, busy, spinning life. So...

❏   Just for today...make a decision to begin to ingrain the habit of prayer deeply into your life. If you are not accustomed to praying, begin your prayer habit by setting aside just five minutes for prayer today.

You can even use your kitchen timer. Then schedule your prayer time. Put it in your daily planner like you do all your other appointments. Next, make a list of things to talk to God about, to talk over with Him. Start with your family. Name them to God one by one, and share your concerns about them.

If you're already in the habit of praying, consider beefing up your commitment. What a privilege it is to pray for others, to be a prayer warrior on behalf of others, to pray around the world for God's people, to be "praying *always* with *all* prayer and supplication in the Spirit, being watchful to this end with *all* perseverance and supplication for *all* the saints" (Ephesians 6:18). You better the lives of others as you pray for them.

❑ Just for tomorrow...set up some kind of system or notebook for keeping records of your prayer concerns. Who would you like to bring before your heavenly Father? What would you like to pray for them? What do you need to pray about personally? What character issues? What family problems? What are the areas where you need God's wisdom? Just make a list, write down the date you prayed, and lift your prayers before God's throne of grace (Hebrews 4:16). Be bold (Hebrews 4:16 again)! And don't forget to leave room on your prayer list for God's answers. Start small...and then watch for the mighty effect of your faithful prayers.

❑ Just for this week...continue to faithfully pray for those people and issues noted on your prayer list.

When a week of faithful prayer passes, increase the amount of time to a measure that indicates growth in this spiritual discipline. As you are faithful to pray and as you see God's answers to your prayers, your faith in Him will be strengthened and your commitment to prayer will grow even stronger. You will definitely want to repeat this wonderful week for life. Wow! Talk about a better life!

Living God's Plan

Developing an effective prayer life isn't as intimidating as most people think. God doesn't care so much about how you pray as long as your heart is right (Proverbs 15:8). God, however, does want you to glorify Him. And you do that when you acknowledge His presence and your dependence on Him through prayer.

God also wants to bless you and grant your requests and all other "good things" (Matthew 7:11). But He asks you to ask. "*Ask* and it will be given to you....For everyone who *asks* receives....Your father who is in heaven give[s] good things to those who *ask* Him!" (Matthew 7:7-11). So go ahead. Ask away. But take heed to this warning regarding your asking...and your heart: "You do not have because you do not ask. You ask and do not receive, because you ask amiss, that you may spend it on your pleasures" (James 4:2-3). Don't be like the coed who disguised her selfish motive with this prayer: "Lord, I'm not asking for myself, but please send my mother a son-in-law!"

Dear heart, let's be serious about prayer. Let's join ranks with God's faithful corps of praying women—wives, mothers and mothers-in-law, daughters and daughters-in-law, grand-mothers, aunts, and co-laborers. Let's remember that "the effective, fervent prayer of a righteous [woman, wife, mother, mother-in-law, daughter, daughter-in-law, grandmother, aunt, and co-worker] avails much" (James 5:16). If it's true that "prayer moves the hand of God," then we, my friend, have work to do—*serious* work! Let's follow the examples and prayer patterns of some of the Bible's heroes of prayer and ask for the right things. Read "The Power of Prayer" that is on the next two pages. Take your time. Think about it. Let it inspire you…and change your prayer life forever!

The Power of Prayer

Moses prayed. His prayer did save
a nation from death and from the grave.
Joshua prayed. The sun stood still,
his enemies fell in vale and hill.
Hannah prayed. God gave her a son;
a nation back to the Lord he won.
Solomon prayed, for wisdom he asked.
God made him the wisest of men for the task.
Elijah prayed with great desire.
God gave him rain, and sent the fire.
Elisha prayed with strong emotion;
he got the mantle and a "double portion."
Jonah prayed. God heard his wail;
He quickly delivered him from the whale.

Three Hebrews prayed, through flames they trod;
they had as a comrade the "Son of God."
Daniel prayed. The lion's claws
were held by the angel who locked their jaws.
Ten lepers prayed, to the priests were sent;
Glory to God! They were healed as they went.
The thief who prayed—for mercy cried;
he went with Christ to Paradise.
The disciples kept praying. The spirit came,
with "cloven tongue" and revival flame!
Conviction filled the hearts of men;
three thousand souls were "born again!"
The Church, she prayed, then got a shock
when Peter answered her prayer with a knock!
Peter prayed, and Dorcas arose
to life again, from death's repose.
When Christians pray, as they prayed of yore,
with living faith, for souls implore,
In one accord, united stand—
revival fires shall sweep the land!
And sinners shall converted be,
and all the world God's glory see![2]

*G*od's *G*uidelines for a *B*etter *L*ife

❧ Walk in obedience to God's Word—*"One who turns away his ear from hearing the law, even his prayer is an abomination"* (Proverbs 28:9).

❧ Bring all your concerns confidently before God—*"Certainly God has heard me; He has attended to the voice of my prayer"* (Psalm 66:19).

❧ Remember to pray in times of trouble—*"The eyes of the LORD are on the righteous, and His ears are open to their cry....The righteous cry out, and the LORD hears, and delivers them out of all their troubles"* (Psalm 34:15,17).

❧ Make it a goal to replace worry with prayer—*"Be anxious for nothing, but in everything by prayer and supplication, with thanksgiving, let your requests by made known to God"* (Philippians 4:6).

❧ Cultivate prayer as a ministry—*"Praying always with all prayer and supplication in the Spirit, being watchful to this end with all perseverance and supplication for all the saints"* (Ephesians 6:18).

Little things come daily, hourly within our reach,
and they are not less calculated to set forward
our growth in holiness than are the greater
occasions, which occur but rarely.[1]

The greatest hindrance to our spiritual development—
indeed, the whole hindrance—is that we allow our
passions and desires to control us, and we do not
strive to walk in the perfect way of the saints.

When we meet the least adversity, we are too
quickly dejected and we turn to other people
for comfort, instead of to God.[2]
—Thomas à Kempis

Pursue Spiritual Growth

*H*ow blessed I am to have not just one but a corps of godly, mature women who have discipled and mentored me through my years as a Christian. Many dear saints and sisters have left their fingerprints on my soul and bettered my life. They inspired, admonished, exhorted, and encouraged me, especially through the first few years of my spiritual development. As I came across Titus 2:3-5 in my Bible, I realized that my corps of women were living out and modeling the qualities of the "older women" found in these verses.

Now you might be thinking, *Who wants to be an old woman?* And you're right. No one wants to get old. But I'm not talking about physical age. I'm talking about spiritual age—maturity and wisdom and discipline, the qualities we're aiming at throughout this book that help you and me live out God's plan for us. Like my mentors who had such an impact on my life, you and I should have a goal to become true biblical older women ourselves. A dream-come-true for us would be to become women who have the spiritual qualities needed to help our younger sisters in the Lord. How do we become these mature, wise women who are available as models for others? The answer is through spiritual growth.

A Sure Formula for Growth

To help us understand what it means to be developing and maturing spiritually, I've spelled it out: **G-R-O-W-T-H**.

G—*Give your life to Jesus Christ*. Receiving Jesus as your Lord and Savior is the beginning of spiritual life. It is also the beginning of all spiritual growth. You cannot have growth without life. Nor can you have spiritual growth without spiritual life. Beloved, Jesus is the source of life.[3] Once you become a Christian, the Holy Spirit begins to work in your heart to fulfill God's will and His plan for your life. And God's will is that you grow spiritually.[4] I know I've asked this question before, but are you alive in Christ?[5] Not only wisdom, but your better—and best life—begins in Him! (And if you're not sure you're alive in Christ, see page 35.)

R—*Recognize sin in your life*. I'm always so saddened when I see a child with some sort of growth defect. My heart and prayers go out to the child and his parents because our family has gone through just such an experience. Everyone knows that it's unnatural for something to hinder the normal growth process in a child's physical body. Thank God that He is able to cause all things—even a birth defect—to work together for good (Romans 8:28)! But just as something hinders a child's physical growth, sin for you and me is that "something" that hinders our spiritual growth.

So...what is sin? Sin is any thought, word, or deed that goes against God's standards presented to us in His Word, the Bible. Therefore, to grow spiritually sin must be dealt with. We must be constantly identifying sin and purging it from our lives so it doesn't block our growth as Christians. We are commanded to be "laying aside all malice, all deceit, hypocrisy, envy, and all evil speaking...that you may grow" (1 Peter 2:1-2). This means to treat these sins like you would treat a dirty, filthy, soiled garment. Strip yourself of them! Throw them off! Be done with them!

Then take a few minutes to reflect on the pattern of your life. Are there any glaring sin areas? Are there any flashing red lights of warning? Are there any blips on your growth screen? Are there any unconfessed sins? Any dirty garments? Quickly acknowledge them to God and lay them aside. Let major change begin by dealing with them...and dealing with them ruthlessly. Don't let anything handicap your growth. Confess your sin...and then experience God's wonderful forgiveness and cleansing (1 John 1:9). "Blessed is he whose transgression is forgiven, whose sin is covered" (Psalm 32:1).

O—*Overcome spiritual laziness.* It's frightening that I have so many choices to make each day when I get out of bed. For instance, I must choose to spend some time that day in physical exercise...or choose to let it slide for another 24 hours. (And this is only one of *many* choices I must make each and every day.) Another of those choices involves whether I will...or will not...spend some time reading God's Word.

Well, dear heart, since you and I want to grow spiritually and make the small changes that better our lives, I think we should call our negligent choices exactly what they are—laziness! When we choose not to exercise, we are choosing to be physically lazy. And even more serious, when we choose not to read the Bible, we are choosing to be spiritually lazy. That means we are forfeiting the development of the strength and stimulus and nourishment needed for spiritual growth. And these necessary qualities come from God through His living, powerful, life-changing, growth-producing Word.

The apostle Peter adds this truth about the Scriptures—and about our eagerness: "As newborn babes, desire the pure milk of the word, that you may grow" (1 Peter 2:2). Want to make a small change for a better life? Then renew your commitment to make some better choices about your use of time. Choose to make the best choice—to spend more time with God in His Word.

W—*Work out a method and rate for growth.* What's so wonderful about choosing to grow spiritually is that there are so many good tools available to help you. Depending on your lifestyle, responsibilities, and schedule, different types of study aids are available. For instance, you can start with resources that help you study the Bible by yourself.[6] Or you can choose to get involved in a women's Bible study at your church. Or you can:

- listen to the Bible on tape or CD or to your favorite Bible teacher or preacher.

- view videos of the teaching of God's Word by those who can help you grow as a Christian.

- read Christian books on spiritual life and spiritual growth.

- attend Christian seminars on a variety of topics that will better your life.

❧ start memorizing key Scripture verses.

❧ utilize these practices and then take the next step—find someone to mentor you and help you make the changes that make for a better life.

If you're more mature in the Lord and are tempted right about now to think, *Ho hum, I already know all this and do all these things,* then I have your next assignment: *Decide the rate of growth.* There's growth...and then there is growth! There is always room for more growth! So make another small change. However many minutes you read your Bible now, double it. Whatever you're studying, spend twice the time. Whatever you're memorizing, memorize more. And go a step further and do a study on the verses you're hiding in your heart.

And how about these changes? Instead of attending so many seminars, try teaching one. Instead of yawning at what we're covering here—things you already know—take your incredible knowledge and pass it on to a younger woman in the faith. And here's another challenge—the same man who gave the statistic of "it takes ten minutes a day to read through your Bible in a year" also gave this one: "By spending 15 minutes a day you can read 25 books in a year."[7] How many books have you read so far this year?

Let's make the changes and take the steps to radical growth. Let's be radical! Let's be bold! Life only gets better when we grow.

T—*Try to find a mentor.* As a new believer, I wanted to grow. I knew I didn't know anything. In fact, I was beginning at about minus ten! Therefore I determined to be a learner. So I went looking for someone who knew more than I did. (And believe me, in my baby state, I didn't have to go very far to find someone.) I am eternally grateful to those who patiently worked with me, who gently encouraged my spiritual growth. Some pushed. Some pulled. And some carried me part of the way. I often use the apostle Paul's words whenever I attempt to express my gratitude— "I am a debtor to" these loving saints (Romans 1:14)!

Do you want to grow spiritually? Then look for another woman who has the maturity and experience you need— that biblical "older woman"—and ask for her help. If she's unable to help at this time, ask her to point you toward someone who can. Keep searching. And don't give up! Unfortunately, "so far in the history of the world there have never been enough mature people in the right places."[8] Just maybe *your* growth will make a difference someday in the life of another woman!

H—*Have a long-term mentality about spiritual growth.* Spiritual growth must be a lifelong pursuit. Growth in spiritual maturity is gained moment by moment, day by day, week by week, and year by year. In many ways, spiritual development is a lot like physical exercise. If you stop exercising, it might not show for a while, but one day you'll wake up to find that everything is sagging in all the wrong places and that you've lost some physical strength.

In the same way, you can deceive yourself into thinking you can get along just fine without the Bible, prayer, and discipleship. One day, however, you wake up to a tragedy or a crisis and find you have very little spiritual strength for meeting a personal emergency. Don't put off growth. And don't be sporadic. Dedicate yourself to ongoing spiritual

growth—for life. Maturing comes in the good times to prepare you for the bad times.

Just for Today...

Now, one more time—How do we cultivate a life of spiritual growth? By the exercise of spiritual disciplines...one day
at a time. This ensures that the disciplines become ingrained
in your daily life—a habit that extends for life. So one more
time...

❏ Just for today...ask God to give you a desire for
greater growth. Ask Him to reveal any hindrances to
your spiritual growth. A hindrance could be sin or
it could be sinful people. It could also be a lifestyle
that's too hectic or too busy to allow time for
growth. Any one of these will stifle your growth.
Also create a Bible-reading plan that fits your
schedule. And can you think of a woman who might
mentor you? Begin praying now about calling her.

❏ Just for tomorrow...continue on your reading plan.
Be faithful. Look forward to the growth it will gen-
erate. Dream of growing in the grace and knowledge of your Savior. And dream of passing on what
you're learning to help others—those in your own
family, church, and group of friends and associates.
Continue to pray about calling an older woman and
asking for help. Go a step further and begin a list of
what you'd like her to teach you.

Also, through prayer, identify areas of spiritual
immaturity and laziness. Then ask God for help
from His Word or for wisdom in asking advice from

a spiritually mature woman. As God leads you, do something radical concerning your spiritual growth. What will that be? Be bold!

❏   Just for this week...continue your Bible-reading plan for the week. By the end of your week, call the older woman you've been praying about contacting. At the end of the week ask God to help you recall the truths you studied this week, the ones that changed your life. Continue on the next week and the next, for life. Faithfulness in these small daily steps will quickly amount to something big. So get excited! It's like exercise. When you exercise, you think more clearly. You have more energy. Similarly, when you exercise your spirit, you're more spiritually alert, more discerning of the things that come your way. You'll begin gaining incredible strength and building momentum as you live your better life.

Living God's Plan

When I open my seminars on *A Woman After God's Own Heart,* I usually quote Psalm 33:11—"The counsel of the LORD stands forever, the plans of His heart to all generations." If you and I truly believed this verse, then we would understand why God's Word is so important.

What better *source* of wisdom is there than "the counsel of the Lord"? What better *confidence* can we have than knowing that God's wisdom, "the plans of His heart to all generations," is sufficient and enduring throughout every stage and age of our lives? And what better *legacy* can we leave behind than to pass on God's eternal wisdom to the next generation of women through mentoring?

Spiritual growth betters your life. And spiritual growth betters the lives of those who come in contact with you. So live God's plan! Grow spiritually. You will, in turn, be the source of great strength and hope for those God brings across your path.

God's Guidelines for a Better Life

* Look to God's Word for growth—*"As newborn babes, desire the pure milk of the word, that you may grow thereby"* (1 Peter 2:2).

* Look to the Savior's life as a model—*"Grow in the grace and knowledge of our Lord and Savior Jesus Christ"* (2 Peter 3:18).

* Look to God for the strength and energy you need—*"Those who wait on the LORD shall renew their strength; they shall mount up with wings like eagles, they shall run and not be weary, they shall walk and not faint"* (Isaiah 40:31).

* Look to God for sure success—*"He who gets wisdom loves his own soul; he who keeps understanding will find good"* (Proverbs 19:8).

* Look forward to a lifetime of spiritual growth and usefulness—*"The righteous shall flourish like a palm tree, he shall grow like a cedar in Lebanon. Those who are planted in the house of the LORD shall flourish in the courts of our God. They shall still bear fruit in old age; they shall be fresh and flourishing"* (Psalm 92:12-14).

God's
Plan
for Your
Daily
Life

Take time to work—it is the price of success.

Take time to think—it is the source of power.

Take time to play—it is the secret of perpetual youth.

Take time to read—it is the fountain of wisdom.

Take time to be friendly—it is a road to happiness.

Take time to dream—it is hitching your wagon to a star.

Take time to love and be loved—it is the privilege of redeemed people.

Take time to care for others—it is too short a day to be selfish.

Take time to laugh—it is the music of the soul.

Take time for God—it is life's only lasting investment.[1]

Manage Your Life

*W*hen it comes to time and the lack of it, two time-management experts have this to say: "We so often hear, *I wish I knew how to manage my time better.* Rarely do we hear, *I wish I knew how to manage myself better.* To manage our lives we must then obviously learn to manage ourselves. Actually good time management is the only way we can possibly get more time for the things we *really* want to do."[2] And I would add, the things we really *need* to do!

Where has the time gone?

I'm sure you've asked yourself this question on the many days when your dreams and good intentions have gone up in smoke. The day is over, you're exhausted, and you wonder, *Where has the time gone? And by the way, where is that better life?*

Actually time didn't go anywhere. It's still here. It's still passing at the rate it always does...60 minutes in each hour...1,440 minutes in each day...168 hours in each week. As we seek to change the use of our time, the better question to ask is, How could I have managed my life better in order to use the little time I do have?

I'll get to it when I find the time.

This is another statement busy women are fond of making without thinking of its ramifications. Time isn't hiding from us, waiting to be found. No, time is right in front of us...right now...awaiting our beck and call...intended to be put to wise use. And no, *time* isn't lost. We are the ones who have lost the *use* of the time allotted to us when we fail to take advantage of it for good, better, and best purposes. So when you hear yourself say, "I need help with my time," you are actually asking for help to manage your life by using your time more wisely.

We'll never be able to "manage" time itself, for time has some strange qualities. For instance...

> Time cannot be bought or rented.
> Time cannot be saved—you cannot store, freeze, or can time.
> Time cannot be manufactured.
> Time expands before your baby arrives and contracts after the delivery.
> Time is slower for your children than for you.
> Time is slower for you than for your dentist.
> Time was slower for you as a student than for your teachers.
> Time is slower for you in church than for your pastor.

As you can see, the issue is really life—not time. We need to understand how we can better manage our lives...which will lead us to a better life. Here are some steps for living out God's plan.

Step 1: Own the Management of Your Life

How do we manage our whole life? How do we even get our arms and minds around the concept? One timeless life-management principle is this: *Know your priorities.* And to guide us in this process, God gives some very specific job assignments and priorities in the Bible.[3] I've written at length about priorities in my book *A Woman After God's Own Heart.*[4] But the point here is that owning the management of your life and knowing your priorities is crucial. "Priorities are not just marginal options....They are life determining. One's personality is molded inescapably into the image of his priorities."[5] What a powerful statement about managing and prioritizing your life! If we would simply change the focus of our time, life, and attention onto the few areas God has given us to manage—our priorities—our time would be much more manageable. So take time for the priority areas in your life. Own them...and manage them.

Step 2: Prioritize Your Time

Time with God—We've covered this before, but God is to be our ultimate priority. Like Jesus said, when we "seek first the kingdom of God and His righteousness," all the other "things" in our lives will fall into place (Matthew 6:33). Thus the better life!

Be sure you change the daily management of your time to reflect God as your first priority. Give Him your early time each day before the family is up and the day—along with your time—gets used up. Give Him your first time, the first fruits of each new and glorious God-given day.

Time with your husband—If you're married, your time with your husband is next in importance. Your husband is a gift from the Lord. Thank God for him and take seriously your God-given assignment to love your husband (which requires time) and to serve your husband (which requires time). Take your cue from the Proverbs 31 wife—"She does him good and not evil *all the days of her life*" (verse 12). Now that's a lot of time devoted to a priority!

Time with your children—Your children are the next priority on God's list. Your time with your little ones during their growing-up years goes so quickly. Don't miss out on this season and stewardship from God. And don't stop giving time to your children after they leave the nest. Plan to spend time with them in their homes. And whatever you do, don't stop with your children. Your grandchildren need as much of your time as you can give them. Again, that's a lot of time devoted to a priority!

Time for family and friends—Absence does not make the heart grow fonder when it comes to family and friends. You have a responsibility from God to love and care for your parents, which again takes time. You also need to cultivate meaningful relationships with your siblings. You've gone through a lot together during the growing-up process, so don't lose contact with them. They are part of your heritage. They are part of your life and should be a part of your children's lives as well.

And don't forget your friends. They need some of your time. But watch out—the problem with some women is they short-change and neglect their husbands and families and focus their time on their friends and work associates instead. Your friends need your fellowship, but not at the expense of your family.

Time for yourself—Have you ever thought of your life as being like a battery that needs to be recharged on a regular basis? Your life is also like a flower that unfolds with the passing of time. Likewise, when you plan in time for yourself to grow spiritually, to develop your spiritual gifts, to define and refine your talents, and to grow as a person, you are recharging and unfolding. You are preparing yourself to bless others. If you want to have an influence on others, plan time for yourself. Be sure you *"grow* in the grace and knowledge of our Lord and Savior Jesus Christ"* (2 Peter 3:18).

Time for the unexpected—I confess! Here's where I fail regularly. I'm sure you're familiar with Plan A and Plan B. Plan A is the plan you make for your day...when you are sane and "things" are sane. In other words, if everything went without a hitch, your day would follow Plan A and become your perfect dream day come true. Plan B is your backup plan. It's the plan you're so often forced to move to because of the unexpected, the unplanned, the surprises, or what I'm learning to accept as "the God factor."

Here's what usually happens. You get up, you have your time with the Lord, and you make your sparkling Plan A. Then you move out on your Plan A day. Things are going well...until the telephone rings and you learn that someone is sick and needs a meal for that evening. Or your husband left something important at home and needs you to bring it to him. Or your child is sick at school and needs to be picked up. Suddenly, whether you like it or not, and whether you planned for it or not, you've moved on to Plan B. And that's O.K. because you've learned to view such Plan B scenarios as opportunities from the Lord for you to serve someone else. You've also learned to expect and cope with the unexpected. Therefore you quickly and quietly—without fuss or complaint—move to Plan B. Oh, to be like Jesus in this grace! He shows us perfectly the grace of handling inter-ruptions (see Matthew 9:18-26). And His way is the better way—the better life we desire.

Time for planning—How can you make time work for you, rather than becoming its slave? By planning. You must spend a short time each day thinking and praying about today and tomorrow. It also helps to allot another period of time weekly to thinking about the week ahead. Also each quarter, half-year, and year, try to retreat and plan for the upcoming segment of your time and your life. You want it to be better, and planning will help.

Time for work—What I mean by "work" here is a job or occupation outside the home. I know you work. (What woman doesn't?) After all, you manage a home and possibly a family. Plus you're a chef, gardener, handy woman, chauf-feur, and so forth. You already have a full-time job with just the responsibilities at home! But if you also work outside the home, you *really* need to plan your day. Someone else is demanding eight-plus hours of your time, so you must know how you are going to manage the remaining hours.

Step 3: Learn What's Important

Learn to be more effective—The Bible shows us examples of women who were very effective. One such person I've already mentioned—the woman in Proverbs 31:10-31. As I said earlier, when I read about her life, her time, and her accomplishments, I often marvel, "How did she get it all done?" Well she got it all done because she was *effective*. Some might say she was *efficient*. True, this woman did all her tasks well, and probably with little wasted effort. But more importantly, this woman did the *right* things well. That's effectiveness!

Are you beginning to understand why prioritizing your life and learning what's truly important is so essential? You can do a lot of things in your busy, fast-paced life, and you can do them well. You can be extremely efficient, but...are they the right things, the best things, God's priority things? If you've pinpointed any areas that are not of a priority nature, you need to also...

Learn to eliminate—Ask: *What can be eliminated from my life at this time that is not a priority?* As Solomon observed in Ecclesiastes 3:1-8, life has its seasons. Today you may be a single woman. Next year you may be married. Or now you may be in the season of child-raising. Or you may be like me, in the season of doing all the things I set aside until my children were raised.

The point is, priorities change. So today, in whatever your situation and season, eliminate those things that don't contribute positively and constructively to God's plan and priorities. Make the changes needed. Eliminate what fails to promote His purposes for your life. There are so many activities we do every day that are not essential. They are discretionary, meaning we can choose to do them or not do them. It makes little or no difference. The call is ours. So if you're really serious about the better management of your time and your life and achieving a better life, these secondary things must be eliminated.

Just for Today...

Throughout this book we're focusing in this section on a daily key to living out God's plan and timeless principles one day at a time. And one of those principles is paying careful attention to time. Our *time* is our life! So...

❏   Just for today...evaluate your day at day's end. What did you choose to do that was discretionary and could have been eliminated? Make a list to build on so you can identify the "time bandits" that robbed you of precious minutes and hours. An easy change you'll want to make is to not make the same mistakes. How could you have better lived this day, a day leading to a better life? Again, if you have a journal, write your answers down...in red ink! You are on assignment from God to use your time and your life for *Him*. It's part of His plan for you.

❏   Just for tomorrow...read Titus 2:3-5 and list the ten essentials for better living it contains. Grab your journal and write them down. This is God's Word to you, so embrace these ten principles as priorities. Then plan them into your tomorrows.

❏ Just for this week...set aside a time to evaluate the present week and plan for the next one. With your lists of "time bandits" and God's list of ten essential principles, craft a better "Plan A" for next week. And by the way, plan on your calendar to do this same exercise at the end of next week. You'll be amazed at your better use and management of time as you continue this drill for the rest of the year. At year's end you can praise God for your progress. And then, of course, you'll want to evaluate the year and plan for the next one. This is how a better life takes shape.

Living God's Plan

We've covered a lot, haven't we? Our time, our lives, our priorities, our purposes. But these are vital. The rest of your life is ahead of you, however long that may be. Your life with its minutes, hours, days, and (Lord willing) years is brimming with possibilities. And you want to make sure you're living out God's plan during those minutes, hours, days, and years. The mark of a woman who is living according to God's plan is that she enters each tomorrow with great excitement and enthusiasm. If you make the necessary changes regarding God's plan for your time and your life, you'll live a better life. Why? Because you will be managing your life God's way, therefore you will have the time to take advantage of every God-given opportunity that all your todays and tomorrows hold.

I can hardly wait! How about you?

*G*od's *G*uidelines for a *B*etter *L*ife

❧ Be aware there is a right time and season for everything—*"There is a right time for everything: A time to be born; a time to die; a time to plant; a time to harvest; a time to kill; a time to heal; a time to destroy; a time to rebuild; a time to cry; a time to laugh; a time to grieve; a time to dance; a time for scattering stones; a time for gathering stones; a time to hug; a time not to hug; a time to find; a time to lose; a time for keeping; a time for throwing away; a time to tear; a time to repair; a time to be quiet; a time to speak up; a time for loving; a time for hating; a time for war; a time for peace"* (Ecclesiastes 3:1-8 TLB).

❧ Be careful how you use your priceless time; it's irreplaceable—*"See then that you walk circumspectly, not as fools but as wise, redeeming the time, because the days are evil"* (Ephesians 5:15-16).

Nine-tenths of wisdom consists in being wise in scheduling time.
—PRESIDENT THEODORE ROOSEVELT

What you do today is important because you are exchanging a day of your life for it.

Each day is a little life, and our whole life is but a single day repeated.

Live by a Schedule

*G*od is a gift-giving God. And a gift He gave me some time ago was a most special friend with a passion for flower arranging. One piece of life-changing advice this dear woman passed on to me was shared in the context of a wedding. We were both busy at work in the kitchen of the church we attended. I was organizing the wedding reception, and Julie was putting together the floral centerpieces for the reception tables. She had all the fresh flowers she was using organized by size and color and laid out on newspapers spread the full length of the kitchen.

And what fantastic centerpieces were coming together before my very eyes! I'd certainly never seen anything like them. As Julie busily snipped and stripped, wired and fussed over each stalk and blossom, I verbally admired the dramatic sprays that somehow magically took on a life of their own under the direction of her hands. From the chaos of the mess in the kitchen, beauty was emerging. Finally I asked Julie why her arrangements were so extraordinary. What made them so spectacular? What was her secret?

In just two words, Julie changed my life. She said, "My motto for everything I do is 'Be bold!'"

Be bold! As we consider a better life and the topic of a daily schedule, I want us to keep Julie's motto in mind. I want us to *be bold*. I want us to *think bold*. And I want us to *live bold* for God. After all, He has given us life in Himself (Ephesians 2:5). He has gifted us to live life for Him (2 Peter 1:3). And He has purposes in mind for our lives (2 Timothy 1:9).

"A List of Projected Operations"

What is a schedule? Technically, a schedule is "a list of times and details of recurring events and projected operations." A schedule is also "a timed plan for a procedure or project." As the "Head of Operations" for your life, your relationships, your home, and your work, you too need a list for the projected operation of these vital spheres of your life. Scheduling is another step for living out God's plan.

Why have a schedule? First there's your purpose—God's purpose. I love the impassioned words of the apostle Paul. When he spoke of God, he added these words—"to whom I belong and whom I serve" (Acts 27:23). To whom do you belong, and who is it you are serving today? A schedule helps you live out your purpose of serving God and of fulfilling His purpose for your life...and your day.

Next there's your manner. A schedule helps to bring more discipline into your life, which better enables you to walk in the Spirit and produce spiritual fruit. When there's no schedule and no plan, stress, frustration, and even rage can characterize the gift of 1,440 sparkling minutes God gives to

Live by a Schedule 97

you each day. We don't know what we're doing...but we know things aren't the way we want them to be. We know we aren't living the better life we yearn for. That's when stressful emotions usually kick in. By contrast, with a schedule—a timed plan for a procedure or project—you can flow through the projected operation of your day in a calm, orderly, smooth progression.

A good schedule is marked by order. For instance, consider again the woman in Proverbs 31. Even a brief look at her daily life (as seen in Proverbs 31:10-31) gives us a list of priorities and a schedule we can follow. Note them both.

- ❧ She feared the Lord (verse 30).

- ❧ She took care of her family and home first (verse 15).

- ❧ She tended her home (verse 27).

- ❧ She served her community (verse 20).

- ❧ She got up early (verse 15).

- ❧ She stayed busy throughout the day (verse 27).

- ❧ She worked into the evening (verse 18).

Creating an Arrangement

Think back to my time with Julie, the creator of bold and beautiful floral arrangements. As she explained to me regarding the masterpieces she creates, some flowers are more brilliant in color, more demanding on the eye, and more important to the visual effect of the bouquet. These major blossoms must be cut tall, stand upright, and be inserted into the arrangement first. Others flowers are softer in color and come next, surrounding the more exciting blossoms. Still others are filler, while some are used for their fragrance. Each bloom, Julie patiently explained, has a place and a purpose.

Before I learned Julie's insights into creating an arrangement of beauty, I used to purchase a cluster of flowers at the grocery store, rip off the cellophane wrapper, and stick it into a vase exactly as it came out of the paper. After Julie's little lesson, I began to treat each flower and its placement as important to the whole. I began to learn how to create an arrangement that was bold and beautiful.

Your day, dear reading friend, is to be treated in the same way and with the same carefulness required in creating a breathtaking floral arrangement. You can have a "bunch" of things you need to do that you stick and stuff into God's gift of 24 hours. Or you can lay out and consider all the different tasks you need to take care of, prepare for, and finish, and then thoughtfully and oh-so-painstakingly prioritize and place them in the perfect position in your schedule.

Don't you think this second way is the better way? As a woman on a mission to live out God's plan for you, you must seriously and prayerfully consider the value of each task and the best time for it...including the value of each minute and the best way to use it. Making this one change in your approach to your day and your duties will better your life.

Creating a Schedule

Step 1—Ask this question first thing each and every day: What is "the one thing," the most important thing, the central focus, the most brilliant "flower" of my day? Once answered, create and build your day around it.

And we know what that determinative flower is, don't we? It's *God*. It's your spiritual life—the one thing that makes all the difference in your day. Without setting aside time to cultivate and nurture the all-encompassing priority of your relationship with God, there will be no bold life lived for God. Without it there will be no energy, no purpose, no wisdom, and no joy. There will be no living out of God's plan...and no better life. "No man is living at his best who is not living at his best spiritually."[1] And this is true for women as well!

So...first things first—schedule your time with God first.

Step 2—Next ask, Who are the people in my life? And be careful how you answer this one. God's list of priorities puts Himself first, then *people*. So, if you are married and have children, they are the priority people in your life, not your sister, best girlfriend, neighbor, or the women at work or church. This doesn't mean that your friends and ministries don't have a place in your life. But when it comes to your schedule, schedule family first...then other people.

Into the schedule (or the "bouquet" of your day) go the people in your life. How can you serve them and tend to them? What will you do for them? And when will you do it? Write your plans down and place them into specific time slots on your daily schedule.

Step 3—Take into account the *future*. Many women's lives are filled with failure and frustration because they neglect this most important step in scheduling their days. Every woman has events and tasks that loom in the future. Lord willing, these activities will one day arrive. Our job is to be ready for them, prepared for them, even eagerly awaiting them. You see, "the plans of the diligent lead surely to plenty" and are advantageous (Proverbs 21:5).

For instance, as I am writing about the scheduling principle, I just took a look at my future. All I can say is, "Eek!" Here's what I discovered: This book manuscript is due in a few weeks, along with its growth and study guide. My little granddaughter Katie is turning three and needs to be properly honored. My family is having its annual reunion over President's Day weekend. Valentine's Day is coming...and you know what that means! Jim and I need to make travel arrangements to various events this spring. And that's just the tip of the iceberg—the biggies.

The future always looks forebidding and impossible. But (I pray!) I've got these items under control. That simply means I've got some part of the work and preparations for each deadline/birthday/reunion/Valentine's Day scheduled on today's schedule. This practice will be repeated each and every day until the day for each important event and occasion arrives...and hopefully I will be ready. (And I didn't even mention April 15, the due date for taxes!)

Step 4—And don't forget *yourself*. Are you trying to lose a pound or two? Are you endeavoring to exercise a little each day? Do you need to pick up the phone and call to enroll in a special class or a Bible study or to make a doctor's or haircut appointment? Do you need to purchase a book you've been wanting to read? Into the daily schedule these worthy endeavors go.

Step 5—After you've become faithful in planning and scheduling your days, you'll want to graduate to creating...

❧ *A weekly schedule*—Especially pay attention to *hor-izontal scheduling*. This is a time-management term for doing the same things every day at the same times...like getting up, reading your Bible, exercising, preparing meals, your daily housekeeping chores, and planning your next day.

Then go to work on your *vertical scheduling*. This term refers to blocking off large time slots during a day...like three hours to clean your house or an hour to work on a correspondence course or run your errands.

❧ *A monthly schedule*—This schedule becomes an appointment calendar-at-a-glance. Key dates, meetings, and commitments are noted so there are no surprises! This practice also brings the big picture of your year down to a smaller, more manageable slice of reality. Now, whose birthday is this month?

❧ *A yearly schedule*—This schedule is a reflection of the flow of your life. It includes birthdays, holidays, family commitments, medical reminders, church events, the school calendar, wedding dates, graduations...and always those deadlines! My yearly calendar includes not only my book deadlines, but my husband's as well. Both of our ministry commitments are written in, plus our anniversary date and Jim's birthday. You'll find our daughters' birthdays there...and now their husbands' birthdays as well (and their anniversaries)...plus those of seven grandchildren. Every holiday and special date is marked off along with my family's annual reunion.

A yearly schedule helps you stay on top of your life…and cuts out a lot of surprises, oopses, bloops, and blunders.

Just for Today…

As you can see, scheduling is a necessity. It's a mirror of your life. It's a tool for improvement. And it's a wand for accomplishment! Think about the creation of the world. God had a schedule…from before the foundation of the world. He knew exactly what He would create each day that first most glorious week of the history of all creation. It was a true masterpiece! And He knew He would rest on the seventh day. How about you? How's your masterpiece looking?

- ❏ Just for today…create a schedule. Spend the first 10 to 15 minutes of your day creating a plan for the day and putting that plan on your daily schedule. And remember—*any* schedule is better than *no* schedule.

- ❏ Just for tomorrow…seek to make a better schedule. Determine to make tomorrow a better day than yesterday. And don't forget to ask God for His wise counsel (James 1:5)!

    Do you really want to have some fun *and* get excited about managing your time and your life? Then schedule a visit to an office supply store. Take time to look at the different types of planners, calendars, and scheduling tools. If you don't have one of these devices, purchase one that will get you started. If you already have one, see if there is something better than what you are using.

❏ Just for this week…make a schedule first thing every
day. Determining a schedule and imposing deadlines give urgency to activities that might otherwise
drag. Keep your journal handy too because you'll
want to record your amazing progress. After all, a
complete makeover is in motion—a makeover that
will make for a better life!

Living God's Plan

As I think about the days of our lives, I can't help but feel
an urgency. Dear reading friend, I'll say it again—all you
(and I) have is today! Only this one day to live out God's
plan. Therefore as you change your mindset and attitude
about the value and importance—and urgency—of each
day, you will move closer to living out God's plan for you.
And as you move into action and fine-tune each day, making
the small changes suggested throughout this chapter, you'll
realize your better life…now!

Pray over your day of potential. And pray through it. And
pray at the end of it. How desperately we need God's clear
direction and assistance for our one day! Without it we won't
care about the day…or about others. We'll indulge ourselves,
shirk our work, and spend God's golden minutes on the
foolishness of this world. And, as the saying goes, "You
cannot kill time without injuring eternity."

As weak and fleshly mortals, we have no hope but to
pray. We must ask God for His guidance and His plan for the
use of our day…which is His. There's no other way our day
will be used for His purposes and glory. And there's no other
way to live God's plan, to bless others, and to move forward

and "press toward the goal for the prize of the upward call of God in Christ Jesus" (Philippians 3:14).

What's in a Day?

Just for today, I will...

Like Enoch—walk in daily fellowship with my Heavenly Father.

Like Abraham—trust implicitly in my God.

Like Job—be patient under all circumstances.

Like Joseph—turn my back on all seductive advances.

Like Moses—choose to suffer rather than enjoy the pleasures of sin.

Like Caleb and Joshua—refuse to be discouraged because of numbers.

Like Gideon—advance, even though my friends are few.

Like David—lift up my eyes to the hills from which comes my help.

Like Jehoshaphat—prepare my heart to seek the Lord.

Like Daniel—commune with God at all times and in all places.

Like Andrew—strive to lead others to Christ.

Like Stephen—manifest a forgiving spirit toward all who seek my hurt.

Like Paul—forget those things that are behind and press forward.[2]

*G*od's *G*uidelines for a *B*etter *L*ife

❧ Be sure to pray before you make your plans— *"Commit your works to the LORD, and your thoughts will be established"* (Proverbs 16:3).

❧ Add structure to your life—*"Ponder the path of your feet, and let all your ways be established"* (Proverbs 4:26).

❧ Plan ahead and reap God's blessings—*"The plans of the diligent lead surely to plenty, but those of everyone who is hasty, surely to poverty"* (Proverbs 21:5).

❧ Always allow for Plan B, God's plan!—*"A man's heart plans his way, but the LORD directs his steps"* (Proverbs 16:9).

❧ Seek to live an ordered life—*"Let all things be done decently and in order"* (1 Corinthians 14:40).

"What makes a home?"
I asked my little boy.
And this is what he said,

"You, Mother,
And when Father comes,
Our table set all shiny,
And my bed,
And, Mother, I think it's home
Because we love each other."

You who are old and wise,
What would you say
If you were asked the question?
Tell me, pray?

Thus simply as a little child, we learn
A home is made from love.
Warm as the golden hearth fire on the floor,
A table and a lamp for light,
And smooth white beds at night—
Only the old sweet fundamental things.
And long ago I learned—
Home may be near, home may be far,
But it is anywhere that love
And a few plain household treasures are.[1]

Care for Your Home

*T*omorrow will be the one-month anniversary of my dear sweet mother's death at age 93. I still can't believe it! Between Jim and me, she was our last living parent. And now, as of New Year's Eve, she is gone. It is a sore loss.

Yet as I've been reminiscing this past month on my growing up years, there's no doubt that my mom marked my life forever as a "home" maker. Although she was a serious and dedicated schoolteacher by day, she was a homemaker *par excellence* at all other times. She loved to sew by hand and by machine. She personally and artistically placed every object in our home to create a sight worthy of a still-life painter's brush. She groomed and tended a plethora of house plants that brought beauty, life, and freshness to our small house. She set the table for every meal with great care—a different tablecloth or attractive placemats, cloth napkins (hand sewn, or rather, in her case, magically "whipped up" out of leftover fabrics). She loved her Blue Willow dishes, and even served the catsup in a small attractive glass bowl with a tiny silver spoon. (No paper plates on our table! And no bottles or jars either!) Every wall, too, was hung with her beautiful and fine needlework, lovingly sewn with her own hands.

Well, I could truly go on and on about my mom (and I'm sure you could do the same about yours). But I shocked myself early this morning as I came down the stairs to begin my new day and caught sight of our breakfast table. There it was, completely set with beautiful woven placemats, every mat with a full place setting of dishes and silverware, complete with a bright cloth napkin in a napkin ring, a live, succulent plant as a centerpiece embedded in a wreath of candles and entwined with twinkle lights. The side table was laden with a bowl of fruit as if a master were about to paint it. I instantly had two thoughts. The first was, *I can't help myself! It's so deeply ingrained in me! I love the beauty of simple things set with care!* And my second was, *Thank you, my dear departed mother! I love you and thank God for you.*

A Home Must Be Built

Two of my favorite proverbs (well, actually four) show me the wisdom of what my mom put into practice regarding her home and homemaking. As you read them, I think you'll agree that small changes on your part will definitely make for a better life for any and all—beginning with yourself—who spend any amount of time under your roof.

- ❦ Wisdom has built her house (Proverbs 9:1).

- ❦ Every wise woman builds her house (Proverbs 14:1).

- ❦ Through wisdom a house is built, and by understanding it is established; by knowledge the rooms

are filled with all precious and pleasant riches
(Proverbs 24:3-4).

🌿 She watches over the ways of her household
(Proverbs 31:27).

What these scriptures communicate is that it's important—
and necessary—to focus on our homes, on the places where
we live. Married or single, we live somewhere. And that
somewhere is to be a home. And that home must be "built"
and watched over. God's Word is making it clear it's part of
His plan for us.

So, my dear reading friend, where is your heart when it
comes to the Home-making and Home-building and Home-
watching Departments? Do you even care? Even a little bit?
A better question is, Do you care passionately? So much so
that you're investing your God-given talents and time to
carry out this important assignment from God? I know from
experience caring about—and taking care of—your home
takes a little doing. But any and every change you make in
this area reaps a better life. Here are a few things that help
me stay focused on home.

Prayer—Coming before God lifts the work of homemaking out of the physical realm and transports it into the
spiritual realm. Prayer moves our hearts to accept God's will
for our lives. Prayer lines up our desires with God's plan for
us. So pray! Pray when you get up. Pray as you plan your
work. Pray that your work will bless the people under your
roof. Pray as you do your work. Pray to finish your work.
Pray to do your work unto the Lord (Colossians 3:23). Pray
when you are done. And as you admire the awesome results
of your handiwork, pray a prayer of praise and thanksgiving

to God. Prayer sweetens—and empowers!—every task. It's a vital first step.

Resolution—This always helps. So purpose in your heart and in prayer to live out God's plan for you. Even if creating and caring for a home is not the burning desire of your heart, purpose to follow God's will, no matter what. Then trust Him for the blessings He chooses to "pour out" and send your way as you obey (Malachi 3:10). Watch for them, wait for them, and write them down when they come. "Forget not all His benefits" (Psalm 103:2). A journal will help you follow this charge.

Presence—Your presence at home is how a home is built, maintained, and enjoyed. It's true that the easiest way to feel at home is to be there. And the more you and I (the home-makers) are there, the more we see, the more we care, and the more time we have to run to our homes. My husband and I travel together—a lot! But the truth is, we are two homebodies. People are so gracious and thoughtful to offer us extended stays, penthouse apartments overlooking a beach, island layovers, getaways for a little R&R, and guided day-tours of their wonderful cities. But the truth is that our hearts are always leaning toward home. So like a pair of homing pigeons, home we fly! Wherever we are, we can't wait to get home!

Don't get me wrong. We greatly enjoy what we do in ministry with God's family everywhere. And we sincerely love those we meet and serve with. And we are truly grateful for all the loving gestures made by Christians. But for us, *home* is where our hearts are. The age old quip is true— "Dry bread at home is better than roast meat abroad!"

Time—Taking time to do what is needed is another key step to caring for your home...or anything else. As I wrote in *God's Wisdom for Little Girls,*[2] regarding a garden,

> The garden of God's little girl—how grand!
> It began with a dream, a prayer, and a plan.
> Nothing this splendid just happens, we know;
> It takes time and care for flowers to grow.

The truth in this simple rhyme applies to a home too. In fact, we could substitute the word "home" for "garden." So dedicate time to taking care of your home—time each day. As you begin to taste the pleasing fruits of your labor, you'll want to commit even more time to your little place called *home*. And soon you'll reap the payoff for your minutes spent—you'll have something grand! And remember, nothing grand or splendid *just happens*. It takes *time* and *care* for a home to grow.

Do you have your dream, your prayer, and your plan? Then all you need is some time! A better life is just around the corner.

A Home Is Built with Care

When I speak of "building" a home, I am not talking about spending money. No, our focus is on the care, for that's how a home is built. What does it take to build a home? It is by wisdom, understanding, and knowledge (Proverbs 24:3-4). It is by ordinary prudence and discretion. It is by skillful management with intelligent and biblical principles. So...

Step 1 would definitely be to possess a blueprint for building a home. (And you do—God's blueprint is right in the Bible). And you need a plan. (And you have that too—God has revealed that too.)

Step 2 would then be to work out God's plan. It's true that one's efforts are usually crowned with success. And it is by your prayer efforts and your work efforts (and by God's good grace!) that your home is built, established, and furnished, that it honors Him and blesses others. When you follow God's perfect plan, your home will be "filled with all precious and pleasant riches" (Proverbs 24:4), "with rare and beautiful treasures" (NIV).

Riches and treasures like what? Like love, joy, peace, goodness—the fruit of the Holy Spirit (Galatians 5:22-23). Like an abundance of spiritual qualities. Like a patient, loving calmness that ministers to body and soul. Like words that are "sweetness to the soul and health to the bones" (Proverbs 16:24). Your home will be founded and furnished when you follow God's guidelines.

Just for Today...

Good habits are purposefully formed. And that's what you want to do today...and every day—form good habits, even (and especially!) in the area of caring for your home. Why? Because what you are at home is what you are. So how about making these small changes toward a better life?

❏ Just for today...spend five minutes praying about your home and homemaking. Pray through the scriptures we've discussed in this chapter. Affirm to

God your desire to build and watch over your home. Then walk through each room. Spend the few minutes that it takes to ensure they're tidy, pleasant, welcoming, and comfortable. Make sure they have a fussed-over feeling. As you pass through each room, think about and pray for each person who occupies that room. Consider his or her needs. Remember the little guy in the poem at the beginning of this chapter, how he remarked on the *people* at home first—"You, Mother...and then Father." Then he went on to convey the importance of the *place*—the set table, his bed (complete with smooth, white sheets), the warmth communicated by the simplest of things...like a table and a lamp. These are some of the small things that make every person's life better.

❏ Just for tomorrow...repeat the daily exercise above. Now add to these gestures of love by thinking about each meal for the day. Consider the health of those in your household, their need for energy and nutrition. Plan meals and snacks for each person. And don't forget to include yourself. After all, it's conceivable that you need the most energy of all. Why? Because *you* are the homemaker. Without you and your efforts, the whole thing topples!

❏ Just for this week...take notice of how you feel as you reap the rewards of "building" and making your home. And if you have a journal, jot down your impressions. One feeling you'll probably experience is some tiredness. But oh, will it be

worth it! Imagine…loving your home for an entire
week, fussing over the people you love and the
place you love for seven whole days, tending to the
little touches that transform a house into a home!
You'll be a week down the road to a better life. And
you'll have much to thank God for!

Also keep a list of improvements you need to
make—not only in your house but in your housekeeping. Note what it was that kept you from doing
your tasks, that drained you of the energy needed to
take care of your high and noble calling of home-
building. Was it food (the lack of, the excess of, the
choice of)? Was it the television? The telephone? Pin-
pointing the culprits will make next week a better
one. One more suggestion—I once heard someone
say, "You become what you read." So purchase or
borrow a book on cleaning your home. Learn a
method that saves you time and gets the job done
quickly.

The truth about all our homemaking efforts is that
we'll be at them for a very long time, right up until
the minute we're no longer able to do the work.
Wherever you live, that place is your home, and that
place becomes the stage upon which you live out
this most important, rewarding, and meaningful
role. Just think of the scores of people you will
bless, not to mention the sheer joy you will receive
from your home-sweet-home!

Living God's Plan

I feel like a cheerleader on the sidelines of your life,
putting all my energy into cheering you on. My encouraging

chants for you and your homemaking go something like this: "Do it! Build it! Love it!... And then do it! Build it! And love it some more!"

But there is one final cheer I want to pass on to you— "Pass it on." If you have daughters and/or daughters-in-law, or if you know younger women in your church, pass on what you know and are learning about taking care of your place. When I visit my two daughters' homes, I'm amazed by their skills, by the beauty they create, by the order I witness in their homes. Why, just yesterday I dropped by to pick up Courtney's little Jacob to take him to his church Cubbies meeting. And what did I see? Courtney's table was set with a red, white, and blue tablecloth (yes, she's a Navy wife through and through!) with placemats for each person. The dishes were already set on the mats. Two tiny candles with little lamp shades were set in the center of the table. And a sprig of evergreen she had plucked from a tree in the back-yard brought its fresh beauty and the energizing scent of pine into her cozy home.

And I'll never forget my Katherine's first Thanksgiving as a married woman. She invited Jim and me to a sit-down dinner of turkey done "Martha Stewart style," artistically arranged and served on a large pewter platter. And there was the table...resplendent with a seasonal runner gracing the length. Katherine had also spread variegated gourds up and down the length of the table, many of them cut out so that lit candles were sticking up out of them. She delighted in using her wedding dishes, silverware, and goblets. To this day I never enter her house without seeing her table deco-rated in a stunning way.

And then I think of my mother...passing on her passion for homemaking to me. And then I think of my daughters...and that's when I hope and pray and thank God that maybe, just maybe(!), I have passed on the same passion to them. And then I think of little Taylor Jane and Katie and Grace, just six and five and one years old, coming along behind my daughters...

As I said, Pass it on! It will better the lives of generations to come.

*G*od's *G*uidelines for a *B*etter *L*ife

❧ Accept God's assignment to create a home—*"The older women [are to]... admonish the young women to [be]...homemakers"* (Titus 2:3-5).

❧ Keep close touch on the affairs of your household—*"She watches over the ways of her household, and does not eat the bread of idleness"* (Proverbs 31:27).

❧ Learning more about homemaking pays big dividends—*"Through wisdom a house is built, and by understanding it is established; by knowledge the rooms are filled with all precious and pleasant riches"* (Proverbs 24:3-4).

❧ Use your energy for positive results—*"The wise woman builds her house, but the foolish pulls it down with her hands"* (Proverbs 14:1).

❧ Realize building a home requires effort—*"Wisdom has built her house, she has hewn out her seven pillars; she has slaughtered her meat, she has mixed her wine, she has also furnished her table"* (Proverbs 9:1-2).

God's
Plan
for Your
Family
Life

Do you take this man to be your lawfully wedded husband, to have and to hold from this day forward, for better, for worse, for richer, for poorer, in sickness and in health, to love and to cherish, till death you do part, according to God's holy ordinance?[1]

Invest in Your Marriage

*J*ust this morning my sweet Jim remarked, "Do you realize we're on the downhill side of the year, moving toward 38 years of marriage?" As the two of us talked about this startling feat, we wondered, How did 38 years together happen? How did we do it? And what have we learned?

How did it happen? Jim and I wholeheartedly acknowledge—100 percent—that an almost four-decade marriage must be attributed to God's good grace and an untold abundance of His transforming power! Whenever we consider the bumpy beginnings of our marriage, we can only fall before Him in complete adoration and thanksgiving.

And how did we do it? I'm chuckling as I think of the obvious answer—We did a lot of it the hard way! But seriously, we have earnestly tried to do it *God's* way. Once we became a Christian family (after eight years on a very rocky road!), we found in the Bible what God had to say about marriage. From that point on we sought to follow the principles for a married couple set down by the Designer of marriage.

And what have we learned? I'm laughing again as this answer pops into my head—a lot! Yes, we've learned an awful lot...and there's still more we're learning every day! But here's a little of what we now know about a better marriage and a better life.

Ten Keys to a Better Marriage

As you read through these principles,[2] keep several things in mind. If you're married, whether to a Christian or non-Christian, these guidelines will help you be a better wife—to be God's kind of wife. They provide roles and goals for you—God's plan for you as a wife. If you're not married, please also take note of the principles. You never know when you will be the one who can help another woman... just because you know God's principles for wives. In the past I helped train college age and career women for short-term summer missions trips. One body of information our church wanted these single women to be able to teach and communicate was God's plan for women in the church and as wives and mothers. You see, God's principles work for every wife...everywhere.

1. *Work as a team*—If your husband or you watches any sports on TV, then you're well aware of the importance of teamwork. And never is this principle more important than in marriage. Teamwork in marriage requires the husband and wife to take up their tandem roles of leading and following. This practice makes a marriage work, thus bettering your life. God asks husbands to lead and wives to follow (1 Corinthians 11:3). Hang on to this principle for now.

2. *Learn to communicate*—Maybe this is a part of the "how" of Principle 1. To function as a team, you and your husband must communicate. That means you must learn how to communicate. More specifically, you must discover how to best communicate with your husband. He's not a woman, so communication with him will not be carried on like it is with your sister, mother, or girlfriends. You'll need to pay attention to *time*—when is the best time to talk to your mate? You'll need to pay attention to *tone*—what is the best tone of voice to use with your husband? And you'll need to pay attention to *tongue*—what is the most gracious and sensible choice of words when talking things over with your hubbie?

The Bible gives us these steps for better communication. Your words are to be...

> ...soft ("a soft answer turns away wrath"—Proverbs 15:1),
>
> ...sweet ("sweetness of the lips increases learning"—Proverbs 16:21),
>
> ...suitable ("pleasant words are...health to the bones"—Proverbs 16:24),
>
> ...scant ("in the multitude of words sin is not lacking"—Proverbs 10:19), and
>
> ...slow ("be swift to hear, slow to speak, and slow to wrath"—James 1:19).

3. *Enjoy intimacy*—Physical communication is a key principle to marriage. Sexual intimacy in marriage was designed by God. Why? Here are some why's and how's.

Proclaimed—God proclaimed that you and your husband are to leave your parents and be joined together as "one flesh" (Genesis 2:24-25). God intends the two of you—two individual people—to come together in marriage and sexual intimacy and become a new whole, complete in each other.

Procreation—God desires that the oneness created between a husband and wife in sexual intimacy result in another generation of offspring who will continue to multiply and fill the earth (Genesis 1:27-28).

Pleasure—Sexual intimacy was also designed by God to provide pleasure for both partners (Proverbs 5:15-19). This pleasure thrives as each spouse chooses to serve the other and determines not to deprive one another (1 Corinthians 7:5).

Purity—Sex within marriage is pure (Hebrews 13:4) and provides power against sexual temptation, contributing positively to the purity of both husband and wife (1 Corinthians 7:2).

Partnership—Each marriage partner has a God-given assignment to satisfy the other's physical needs and to see that their own needs are satisfied too (1 Corinthians 7:3-4).

Protection—Sex in marriage is a safeguard against lust, temptation, and Satan's alluring, worldly tactics (1 Corinthians 7:5).

   4. *Manage your money*—My husband writes and teaches on marriage, and one thing I've heard him say many times

is that beneath almost every argument between a couple is some issue over finances. It's true that money—the use of it and the lack of it—can produce tension and sidetrack the better life you are seeking. So what can you as a wife do?

Here's one change that reaps huge rewards: It helps if you are content (Philippians 4:11-13). Contentment enables you to look at something and say in your heart, "I can live with it or without it. It doesn't make any difference to me. I'm content in the Lord." That attitude will go a long way in the Money Department.

The area of finances also creates an opportunity to practice patience, to grow in your trust of the Lord, and to implement good communication skills with your husband. Another step you can take is to determine to grow in your understanding of money management, budgeting, saving, basic bookkeeping, and giving. Get a book on the subject...and start growing!

5. *Keep up the home*—Married or single, your home is an indicator of your spiritual maturity and a direct reflection of your care and character. And if you're married, home is the focal point for your marriage and family. Its condition also sends a loud message and leaves a visual impression on friends, neighbors, and those at church about you, your husband, and the attention you pay (or don't pay) to the people and place that make up your home. This is a vital area for a wife! So treat the upkeep and atmosphere of your home with utmost care. Become a home lover (Titus 2:5). A lot is riding on your desire to keep up your home, including a better life for your family members. Make it your aim to look well to the ways of your household (Proverbs 31:27).

6. *Raise your children*—Here's another area that requires some good relationship skills. The typical scene goes something like this—generally Mom spends time at home with the little darlings, training and disciplining away...and then Dad comes home and proceeds to train and discipline in another way...or not at all. Child-raising is an area of potential friction and, once again, calls for good communication. The goal is to know what the Bible says about child-raising, talk it over with your husband, agree on a plan for raising and training your children...and then be prepared to revise the plan often.[3]

Why? Because things change. You're growing and learning, the children are developing and moving from stage to stage, and the outside influences of others (friends, school surroundings, neighbors, workmates at their jobs, sports teammates, and coaches) are appearing almost daily. Yes, you'll be talking with your husband about these things a lot, maybe even every day...and for a long time. So don't forget God's keys to good communication (see Principle 2). You are to train your children and bring them up in the ways of the Lord (Proverbs 22:6 and Ephesians 6:4). That's God's plan, and living out that plan requires that you and your husband communicate, agree, move forward together, and adjust along the way.

7. *Make time for fun*—Jim and I work hard...*very* hard. But we make it a point to make time for fun. We regularly schedule in recreation and time spent on our hobbies and interests, whether joint or individual ones. We adore our walks in the woods, kayaking as a couple, and boating when the weather permits. Fun for us is scouring flea markets and

junk stores for used treasures. Fun is walking through the lobbies of hotels we could never afford to stay in. (And *real* fun is to have coffee in such a hotel, to sit and sip...and enjoy the magnificent ambience for the price of two cups of coffee!) What is fun for you and your husband? Is it jigsaw puzzles? Bicycling? Do you perhaps need to do a little more communicating with your husband on when, how, and what you can do to make time for fun? After all, your better life should include some fun as a couple!

8. *Serve the Lord*—Nothing is more healthy for a couple than serving the Lord together. Along with your regular worship at church, such service is good for you because it focuses the two of you outside of yourselves and onto bettering the lives of others. As a couple, Jim and I have set up, cleaned up, and washed up more times and more dishes at the church than we can count. We've stuffed, assembled, painted, planted, cooked, moved, visited, given, served, hosted...you name it, we've done it in both our church and our community. How can you and your husband serve the Lord and His people?

9. *Reach out to others*—Hand in hand with serving the Lord is reaching out to others. What a wonderful privilege you and your husband have to work together as you minister to your friends and neighbors. By seeking to apply the other nine of these timeless principles for marriage, the two of you model the reality of Christ and a Christian marriage before an unbelieving world. As you open your heart and your home in hospitality to others and their children, you demonstrate Christ's love to all who enter through your doors.

Just for Today...

There you have it—nine (I've saved one for later!) out of ten guidelines for you and your marriage! It's a lot to think about, isn't it? And to apply...because nothing as grand as a good marriage ever happens without work. Each principle is part of God's plan for strengthening your marriage. So pick out several of God's principles or "steps" and begin to make them a part of your marriage. And be prepared—more than likely you'll notice some changes.

❏ Just for today...review the nine principles and the one that follows. Write out all ten on a 3" x 5" card. Carry them with you and revisit them often, even every hour. Do as Solomon said: In essence, "Bind them around your neck, write them on the tablet of your heart" (Proverbs 3:3). Then go a step further and identify the one principle that troubles you most, that causes you to stumble, that is perhaps a source of contention between you and your husband. Pray...and purpose to zero in on it. It will change you and your marriage.

❏ Just for tomorrow...get your gray matter perking! Can you cook your husband's favorite meal? Can you drop a little love note into his sack lunch or slip it into his pocket or backpack or briefcase? Can you think of three things you can compliment him on...and can you verbalize them?

   Can you plan a romantic evening together after the children are in bed? Think! Plan! Act!

❑ Just for this week…read through this acrostic on marriage each day, paying attention to its instruction and your heart's response.

M—make your marriage a priority.
A—ask God for wisdom.
R—respect and honor your husband.
R—realize marriage is a book with many chapters.
I—invest large amounts of time in your marriage.
A—adhere to God's keys to communication.
G—grow in your understanding of your role as a wife.
E—enjoy your mate and God's gift of marriage!

Living God's Plan

And now for the greatest of all keys to a better marriage! Be sure you…

10. *Grow in the Lord*—The greatest influence you can have on your marriage is through your spiritual growth. As you grow in the Lord, you become a tremendous support to your husband as you are available to listen, encourage, and give wise counsel. Even if yours is a difficult marriage and even in difficult times, your growth in the Lord will give you the wisdom for handling problems. Your spiritual growth permeates every area of your life. It's vital to your husband and the well-being of your marriage and family. So make the changes that will make you more like the woman in Proverbs 31, who honored the Lord and was highly praised and appreciated by her husband (Proverbs 31:28-30). The best way to enjoy a better marriage is to continually grow in the Lord.

*G*od's *G*uidelines for a *B*etter *L*ife

❧ Guard against anything that would divide you as a couple—*"Therefore a man shall leave his father and mother and be joined to his wife, and they shall become one flesh. Therefore what God has joined together, let not man separate"* (Genesis 2:24 and Matthew 19:5-6).

❧ Concentrate on helping your husband—*"And the LORD God said, "It is not good that man should be alone; I will make him a helper comparable to him"* (Genesis 2:18).

❧ Whatever you do, do with a team mentality—*"Two are better than one, because they have a good reward for their labor. For if they fall, one will lift up his companion"* (Ecclesiastes 4:9-10).

❧ Make sure everyone knows how much you love your husband—*"Let the wife see that she respects her husband"* (Ephesians 5:33).

❧ Keep the fire of passion burning—*"Let the husband render to his wife the affection due her, and likewise also the wife to her husband"* (1 Corinthians 7:3).

A mother whose heart is obedient to God, full of faith,
and dedicated to the Lord and to her family will dedicate
her time, energy, and life to taking full advantage
of the opportunity to train her children and
fulfill her parental duty to do so.

—Elizabeth George

Train Your Children

During many years of our marriage, my husband has spent a great deal of time away from our home. Jim's involvement with missions, his monthly duties in the U.S. Army Reserves, his responsibilities as pastor of visitation, evangelism, and outreach, plus his night classes at seminary and teaching in a Bible institute, added up to many absences...which added up to my often being home alone with our two daughters during their formative years.

So what's a young mom to do?

Wisdom from a Godly Mother

As I searched for help on how to handle my two little preschoolers when their dad was away, I turned to reading the many biographies of Ruth Graham, wife of Billy Graham. I had heard that during some of the years of their marriage, the great evangelist Billy Graham was away from home for months at a time. Surely Mrs. Graham had practical help she could give me for those times when my Jim was gone.

And so I read. And as I read, I learned...that Mrs. Graham was a lover of the book of Proverbs...that she read Proverbs

133

daily...that she gleaned principles from the Proverbs for raising her children...that she kept her Bible, opened to Proverbs, on the kitchen table all day every day...that she visited the kitchen table often each day to seek God's wisdom whenever she needed help for handling her five children without the assistance of her husband.

Wisdom from God

Taking a page out of Mrs. Graham's book, I turned to my Bible, to the book of Proverbs. Each day when I read the "Proverb for the Day" (as we discussed in chapter 4), I specifically looked for proverbs that spoke of mothers and mothering, of parents and parenting, of children and child-raising. To this day, the verses I found are clearly marked in my Bible (although the decades have definitely dulled the pen markings). They guided my daily life as a young mom with a houseful of little tykes and toddlers who became tweens and teens. And they are still a living part of me as my two daughters, now young moms with preschoolers, are using the same principles!

So if you're a mom in need of a few steps for better parenting (and what mom isn't!), here's the first four of what I call...

Ten Keys to Confident Child-Raising

1. *Teach your children*—Not only does this principle for mothers come first in the Proverbs (1:8), but it comes often! I counted at least 20 times where some form of parental teaching is mentioned in the book of Proverbs.

God is not expecting you to have a teaching degree, credentials, or experience. But He is most definitely expecting you to teach your children. It's part of His plan for you and your family. In fact, teaching almost appears to be the Number One duty of a Christian parent. The Bible instructs, If you love your children, discipline them (Proverbs 13:24). But it also indicates that if you love your children, *teach* them. And like discipline, the earlier the better!

I would also say, "Teach them, no matter what!" Moms tell me all the time, "But my children don't want to have devotions. They don't want to sit and listen to me read the Bible or Bible storybooks."

Dear mom, my answer is always the same—"Give your children what they need, not what they want." You're the mom. You're the adult. You know what's best and what groundwork needs to be laid for the future. Teaching your children gives them a base of information (God's truth) from which they can live their lives (God's way). It equips them to function throughout life with wisdom. It helps them avoid many mistakes and heartbreaks. And that makes for a better life for them. So make sure that your children "hear the instruction of...the law" or *Torah,* meaning the law of God, the Word of God (Proverbs 1:8 and 6:20). And see how much fun you can have as you learn together.

2. *Train your children*—"Train up a child in the way he should go, and when he is old he will not depart from it" (Proverbs 22:6). That's God's Word to His moms. So my thinking goes like this—*God says to train them, therefore I train them!*

The usual interpretation of this proverb is that if a parent trains a child properly, that child will choose the path of God in later life. Of course there are exceptions, but the principle still stands. So first of all, we mothers obediently, by faith, train our children. And we train them first in God's way. From that point on, we also train them along the lines of their natural talents and individual inclinations or bents.

And what does "training" require of a mom? First of all *a heart of obedience,* a heart that will do the work of training up her children.

But it also requires *a heart of faith.* As a mom after God's own heart, you have to believe that no matter how dark and discouraging things get or how many mysterious, heart-breaking turns the parenting path takes, your teaching is important…because God says it is.

And it takes *a heart of dedication.* This is one of the translations of the word "train"—"dedicate" your child and your house and household to the Lord,[1] and when the child is old, he will not depart from Him.

So no matter what—no matter what the obstacles, no matter what the lack of "payoff," no matter how tired you are, no matter if there isn't even a glimmer of hope, no matter if your diligent teaching and training seems to be making no difference—a mother whose heart is obedient, full of faith, and "dedicated" to the Lord and to her family will dedicate her time, energy, and life to training her children.

3. *Instruct them*—That's the instruction of Proverbs 10:1: "A wise son makes a glad father, but a foolish son is the grief of his mother." (As one commentator interjects, "Every son may turn out to be a Paul or a Judas, with all that means by way of joy or grief.")[2] So what, we wonder, should a mother and father pass on to their children so they become wise and not foolish, so they can have a better life too? Solomon points specifically to instruction in the area of work.

He who has a slack hand becomes poor, but the
hand of the diligent makes one rich. He who gathers
in summer is a wise son; he who sleeps in harvest is
a son who causes shame (Proverbs 10:4-5).

Solomon is saying that a wise adult is one who's overcome laziness and carelessness and learned to be diligent
and aggressive in his or her work. A mature person knows
when to work and how to work, when to pour it on and
when to relax, how to seize the day and the opportunities it
brings, and how to begin a project, how to make steady
progress, and how to finish. The person who follows the
biblical work ethic experiences the sweet taste of success
and the rewards of diligent labor.

Therefore, dear diligent mother, teach your children diligence versus laziness, to work versus to shirk, to finish
versus to merely dream and dawdle, to march versus to
meander, to focus versus to dabble. And just how does a
mom move her child in this direction? By...

> ...communicating clearly what the chore or work or
> job is that must be done,
>
> ...assigning work that is age-appropriate,
>
> ...giving specific instructions about what is expected
> and any time lines or deadlines involved,
>
> ...training and showing her child how to do the job,
>
> ...insisting that the work meet a set standard,
>
> ...requiring that a job be done again if it doesn't meet
> the set standard,

...reviewing instructions each time a job is given,

...making sure the job is finished,

...asking for a verbal report,

...checking it out herself,

...fine-tuning the "loose ends,"

...rewarding (with praise, with applause, with smiles and hugs or high-fives, with a break, with bragging to others, with a handwritten note of praise on the pillow or desk, with a star on a poster or with car privileges, depending on age, with food as in "we'll have snack time after you've put your toys away," with fun as in "we'll go to the park or go swimming..." or "you can go visit your friends when you've finished your homework").

Perhaps your diligent efforts in teaching your children a strong work ethic will lead them to one day declare along with John Wesley, the founder of Methodism and a man marked by his dedication to God and to hard work, "Leisure and I have parted company. I am resolved to be busy till I die."[3]

4. *Correct them*—There's no way to miss this loud message from the Bible. Proverbs shouts to every parent, "He who spares his rod hates his [child], but he who loves him disciplines him promptly" (13:24). "Chasten your son while there is hope" (19:18) (and I like to imagine an exclamation point of urgency here!). In correcting your children you are following in the footsteps of your heavenly Father, "for whom the LORD loves He corrects, just as a father the son in whom he delights" (3:12).

And why are you to correct your children? First and foremost because God says you should. Again Proverbs cries out and commands, "Do not withhold correction from a child" (23:13). Also because "foolishness is bound up in the heart of a child; the rod of correction will drive it far from him" (22:15). "The rod and rebuke give wisdom, but a child left to himself brings shame to his mother" (29:15).

Dear mom, it's hard to grasp—and even harder to follow through—but we actually do our children a disservice when we fail to correct and direct them. You see, when we fail to discipline, we are actually choosing to raise a fool, to sentence him or her to a life of pain, uncontrolled emotions, stupidity, agony, and harsh consequences. For a better life, however, God says to moms:

- discipline your children,
- discipline early in their lives,
- discipline faithfully and consistently, and
- discipline out of a heart of love.

Count on it—your children will protest, cry, squirm, and argue. That's normal. And prepare for it. It's something else a keen mom does. But remember, a wise mother doesn't let whining or angry kids unnerve her or rock her decision to correct wrong behaviors. Solomon encourages us that while the child may cry, "he will not die" (Proverbs 23:13).

Just for Today...

Teaching. Training. Instructing. Correcting. Sounds like a lifelong challenge, doesn't it? And it is! But these assignments from God make for a better life for you *and* for your children. Fortunately, these skills are gained one day at a time. So what can you do…just for today? I'll include more suggestions at the end of chapter 12, but here are a few quick in-and-out applications.

- ❏ Just for today…pick a time, a place, and a portion of the Bible to read out loud with your children.

- ❏ Just for tomorrow…prepare yourself to follow the list of "instructions" that start on page 137 for training your children in the fine art of working with diligence.

- ❏ Just for this week…talk about correcting your children with your husband. If there's no father in the family, seek the counsel of your pastor or an older woman. Also visit your Christian bookstore and choose one book about child-raising.

Living God's Plan

I love every mother of children who range from babies to high schoolers. In fact, I love all women. But somehow this group of moms is so refreshing. Why? Because they're so teachable. There's nothing proud about them. And there's nothing lazy about them. And they have a definite need to know more! There's a hunger for help and information. They are truly *in* the race and *running* the race—every minute of every day. They live every second where the rubber meets the road. Theirs is a day-in, day-out struggle to discover principles, methods, skills, and practices as they seek to raise the world's—and God's—next generation. They truly have hearts that are seeking the changes that will make for a better life all around.

Are you one of these need-to-know moms? I pray that what I've shared from God's Word gives you the courage to continue on, to get up just one more time, just one more day, to look up to our Lord for His strength and wisdom (Proverbs 3:6 and James 1:5), and to persevere by faith, knowing that you're doing what's right because God asks it of you. Take heart...and take up God's calling to you.

Or perhaps you are older and wondering, *Well, this chapter has nothing for me. I've already raised my children. When is this woman going to have something to say that applies to my life?*

Well, I do have something to say to you (and to me, too, as a mother of two married daughters and a grandmother of seven). Only it's not from me—it's from God. In the Bible God has this to say to women like you and me: As "the older women" in the church, we are to teach and "admonish the young women to...love their children" (Titus 2:3-4). God is calling us, His older, wiser, more experienced moms, to pass on what we know about raising children. If you answer His call, you'll be a hero...and a lifesaver, too, as you better the lives of others.

Or perhaps you're single. Do you have nieces and nephews? Are there children in your church? Do any of your friends have kids? Just look at the opportunities you have to use these principles!

God's Guidelines for a Better Life

❧ Take every opportunity to teach your children about God—*"And these words which I command you today shall be in your heart. You shall teach them diligently to your children, and shall talk of them when you sit in your house, when you walk by the way, when you lie down, and when you rise up"* (Deuteronomy 6:6-7).

❧ Do your best...and trust God with the results—*"Train up a child in the way he should go, and when he is old he will not depart from it"* (Proverbs 22:6).

❧ Be sure you're living out what you're teaching—*"My son, give me your heart, and let your eyes observe my ways"* (Proverbs 23:26).

❧ Use parenting methods that produce positive results—*"Do not provoke your children, lest they become discouraged"* (Colossians 3:21).

❧ Remember your faithful instruction lays the groundwork for your child's salvation—*"Continue in the things which you have learned and been assured of, knowing...that from childhood you have known the Holy Scriptures, which are able to make you wise for salvation through faith which is in Christ Jesus"* (2 Timothy 3:14-15).

There is no nobler career than that of motherhood
at its best....There is no higher height to which
humanity can attain than that occupied by a converted,
heaven-inspired, praying mother.[1]

—ELISABETH ELLIOT

Love Your Children

A promise is a promise. And in the last chapter I promised you ten keys to confident child-raising… and here are the rest. So far we've learned steps that include teaching, training, instructing, and correcting our children. Let's continue.

5. *Cherish them*—From beginning to end, Proverbs shows us this tender quality in the heart of a mother toward her sons and daughters. For instance,

- Solomon, the writer of most of the proverbs, described himself as well-loved, his mother's darling, an object of her tender, loving care, as "tender and the only one in the sight of my mother" (Proverbs 4:3).

- The mother in Proverbs 31:2 said, "What, my son? And what, son of my womb? And what, son of my vows?" Not only does this cherished son matter to his mother, but he matters so much that she's vowed him to God.[2] Her words tumble forth and each phrase adds to the intensity of her emotion.[3] Her child (personally) is a child from her own body (physically) and has been dedicated to God (spiritually).

❧ In 1 Samuel 1 we meet Hannah, who wanted a child so badly she wept and could not eat (verse 7). She declared to God in agonizing prayer, "If You will...give Your maidservant a male child, then I will give him to the LORD all the days of his life" (verse 11).

Two things call out to moms from these scriptures. From the *child's* perspective, each must know in his own heart of his special place in his mother's heart. Does each of your children know that he or she is cherished, well-loved, and precious to you? And from the *mother's* perspective, each of your children should be dedicated to God. Has your love grown to become the greatest love of all, a love that dedicates your cherished ones to God?

6. *Take care of them*—You might be shocked to learn how many Christian moms are lax in this area of TLC (tender loving care). But providing daily care for your children is definitely God's plan for your life as a mom. Plus it's another way that we follow God's pattern of love. God feeds us as His children, clothes us, gives us what we need to drink, and gives us rest (Matthew 6:25-32 and 11:28)...and we should do the same for our children. Also, a look at the life of the mom in Proverbs 31 shows us that her daily tasks included providing and giving food to her household (verse 15) and seeing to their clothing needs (verse 21).

I know from firsthand experience that sometimes dispensing TLC is the last thing we want to think about in our busy, helter-skelter days. But as a mom-in-the-making, I had to learn to turn things around. I had to change. For instance, instead of waiting until the last minute to think about meals and menus (or which drive-through to use or pizza delivery to call!), I began to do it first. In the morning I planned the day's meals. Another change was beginning food preparations early in the day. God knows what we need, and He follows through and provides it. And I tried to do the same. Believe me, this was a small change that made for better lives for my children and a less hectic home life!

(And P.S.—Another change I made was to plan my meals and make a grocery list for the entire week on Sunday afternoons, with my planner, grocery list, and recipe box in hand.)

7. *Pay attention to them*—Often it's hard to pay attention to our children. We're soooo busy! There's soooo much to do. And in some cases, there are so many children to take care of that we fail to pay enough attention to them. And it's also true that if we don't, our darlings will somehow, someway, at some time, let us know it.

But a number of proverbs point out that we need to consciously pay attention to our children's development and to their friends. Why? Because telltale behaviors signal to parents exactly what's going on...and they are right in front of our noses! All we have to do is pay attention to them. Learn from these proverbs:

> "Even a child is known by his deeds, whether what he does is pure and right" (20:11). There are no surprises in the character development of our children...if we're paying attention. The basic nature of a person reveals itself

early in life. Therefore, open your eyes, mom! What's he or she up to?

"Be diligent to know the state of your flocks, and attend to your herds" (27:23). Like the care and diligence of a good shepherd, you should be even more diligent in your watchcare over your sheep, your flock, your children.

"Whoever keeps the law is a discerning son, but a companion of gluttons shames his father" (28:7). Who are your children's best friends? Others who obey God's law...or fools and good-for-nothings? Pay close attention to the friends your child runs with.

"The rod and rebuke give wisdom, but a child left to himself brings shame to his mother" (29:15). The standard interpretation of this proverb teaches that children who grow up with discipline become wise, while children who are left to themselves to do as they like or to figure things out for themselves are doomed to be foolish, undisciplined adults. Be sure to seek the opposite result: "Correct your [child] and he will give you rest; yes, he will give delight to your soul" (29:17).

8. *Promote peace in your home*—Here's a child-raising principle that bailed me out of many a squabble between my two girls. It takes some doing, but the peace is worth it. I call these "The Three C's" for peace in the home: Cast, Correct, and Cast again.

"*Casting lots* causes contentions to cease, and keeps the mighty apart" (Proverbs 18:18). In the days when Proverbs was written, casting lots was a way of determining God's will and settling matters between parties.

Today moms often have to settle matters between brothers and sisters. Well, I applied the principle of casting lots through the age-old practice of drawing straws. For instance, is there an unpleasant work chore that someone must do? Or is one bowl of ice cream a wee bit larger than the others? Are the clamors of family members rising as they express what they believe to be right or fair? When you cast lots or draw straws, everyone has a fair chance and contention ceases. Your reward is a peaceful settlement between siblings who might otherwise resort to force...or at least to forceful yelling.

"*Correct* your [child], and he will give you rest; yes, he will give delight to your soul" (Proverbs 29:17). In other words, a child who's disciplined properly will bring joy and rest to your heart instead of anxiety and heartache. If tension is mounting in your home, it's usually a sure sign that someone needs to be disciplined in some way. Your home should be a place of peace. So correct your child and enjoy the peace and quiet and rest that results.

"*Cast out* the scoffer, and contention will leave; yes, strife and reproach will cease" (Proverbs 22:10). Is one of the little ones arguing? Pushing? Picking a fight? Are the sounds of strife rising? Send (or "cast out") the instigator to his or her room for an attitude adjustment. Or sit him or her down in what I called "the waiting chair" for five minutes. While she is waiting (and of course being excluded from family fun!) she can calm down. And if five minutes doesn't do it, up the count on the next round. (And don't forget to use your timer for a multitude of functions in child-raising!)

9. *Require respect from them*—Home is the training ground for life. So start instilling the attitudes and actions you desire from your children at home. And respect is foundational. Teach your children to respect (honor) you and your position of authority as their parent. When a child respects his parents, he will respect all authority, whether at school or later as a grown-up respecting his or her boss and governmental laws in general. And remember, this is the fifth of the Ten Commandments (Exodus 20:12). If a child honors and respects authority, starting with his parents, he will honor all authority and his life will be blessed.

10. *Be patient with them*—"The fruit of the Spirit is... patience" (Galatians 5:22 NASB)...and that's what every mom needs 24/7. You exhibit patience yourself when you...

- Give a soft answer (Proverbs 15:1).

- Study how to answer before you speak (Proverbs 15:28).

- Play-act.

What do I mean by play-act? Here's a typical scene. When my daughters were underfoot day-in and day-out, tension mounted. I used to ask myself, *Now how would a patient mother sound? How would a patient mother act? What would a patient mother say? What would a patient mother do?* I would usually think of one of my mentors and her great patience. Once I stopped and asked questions like these, I would then play-act. I would *do* what the Proverbs said to do and what my mentors taught. I would speak to my girls in a tone of voice I'd heard other wiser (and more patient!) mothers use. I would choose the words and manner exhibited by moms I respected.

Just for Today...

Mothering is for life. If you're a mom, that means you will be practicing these ten principles for child-raising in varying degrees for a long time. So what can you do...just for today?

❏ Just for today...talk to the Lord about your children. Pour out your heart to Him. Share your concerns and inadequacies with Him. Ask for His help and wisdom. Implore Him to show you changes you could make. Purpose to be a mother who prays. Set up a prayer journal or pages for your children in your personal journal. And never forget that "the effective, fervent prayer of a righteous [mother] avails much" (James 5:16)!

❏ Just for tomorrow...set up a time to talk to your husband about your children. Seek to establish standards for the family. Formulate and agree on a list of family standards. The list will change as your children grow and the issues of their lives shift, but there should always be a solid foundation. Write out a few thoughts and share them with your husband. Be open to his thoughts and move forward together. Remember, "two are better than one" (Ecclesiastes

4:9), and it helps to be united in your parenting objectives.

❑   Just for this week…talk to several older and wiser Christian moms. I've already mentioned my corps of older women and advisors, the "older women" God put in my path just when I needed them. They did their part—they taught me how to love my children (Titus 2:3-4). And I did my part—I, as the "younger woman," sought them out, asked for help, and tried to make the changes they suggested. Who will you turn to this week? And here's another question—What books will you begin reading this week to help you as a mother?

Living God's Plan

Actions speak louder than words…and somehow our children seem to especially know this. And because they live with us and witness firsthand our day-in, day-out conduct, they won't listen to us preach something we don't practice. So we must live out genuine faith before our children. It's part of God's plan for us and for our children.

Genuine faith accomplishes two things. First it gives us credibility and a platform for teaching God's Word. And second it gives our children a priceless model of a person who loves God and depends on Him. Do you want your children to love God and follow Him? Then they must see *you* love God and follow Him, His ways, and His plan.

That's what Eunice and Lois did for their little Timothy. This mother and grandmother tag-team shared sincere, genuine faith. They had the real thing and they were the real thing (2 Timothy 1:4-5). And Timothy became the closest companion and friend of the apostle Paul.

Make it your prayer to be the real thing, mom. Make the changes that help you live out these words written about Eunice, the mother of Timothy: "Timothy received...the gift of life twice from his mother. She gave him birth and then showed him what a life of faith could be."[4]

God's Guidelines for
a Better Life

🌿 Accept God's assignment to love your children—
*"The older women...[are to] admonish the young
women to love...their children"* (Titus 2:3-4).

🌿 Enjoy the joy God means you to have as a mom—
*"He maketh the barren woman to keep house, and
to be a joyful mother of children. Praise ye the
LORD"* (Psalm 113:9 KJV).

🌿 View your children as a gift from God—*"Behold,
children are a heritage from the LORD, the fruit of
the womb is a reward"* (Psalm 127:3).

🌿 Don't lose sight of your responsibility as a parent—
*"Do not provoke your children to wrath, but bring
them up in the training and admonition of the
Lord"* (Ephesians 6:4).

🌿 Be sure your children know about Jesus—*"But
Jesus said, 'Let the little children come to Me, and
do not forbid them; for of such is the kingdom of
heaven'"* (Matthew 19:14).

God's
Plan
for Your
Personal
Life

The clothing of dignity stamps [God's woman]
with the Lord's acceptance, as His faithful servant, the
child of His grace, and the heir of His glory.[1]

Cultivate
Inner Beauty

Recently I overheard two Christian moms of preschoolers discussing a talk show they had both watched on television. The program had centered on women—even teenagers—who were obsessed with their appearance. In fact, they were living for the day they could afford (more specifically, charge on their credit cards!) plastic surgery and liposuction treatments to improve and enhance their looks. Now the startling thing to me was not that the two women had watched the program. No, I was shocked that both of these women felt the same way about their looks and appearance as those interviewed on the TV program.

Unfortunately such views about beauty and thoughts of inferiority preoccupy the minds and hearts of many Christian women. But what does the Bible tell us about our appearance? What are God's timeless thoughts on our daily concern of beauty?

Timeless Beauty Tips

1. *True beauty is internal.* Throughout the Bible God focuses on what's inside, not on outward appearance. What is of utmost importance to God is your heart—not your face,

your features, or your figure. So…what's inside? Here's what God has already done to make you beautiful in His eyes.

—You have been *transformed* by God on the inside. Where you were once "dead" in your trespasses and sins, God has made you "alive" together with Christ (Ephesians 2:5). That means you are now "His workmanship, created in Christ Jesus" (verse 10). Talk about beauty!

—You are also *a new creation*. The Bible says "if anyone is in Christ, he is a new creation; old things have passed away; behold, all things have become new. Now all things are of God" (2 Corinthians 5:17-18). Imagine…all the old things—the old standards, the old priorities, the old beliefs, the old loves, and the old value systems—are gone! "In Christ" and as "a new creation" you instead see all things, including the issue of your appearance and looks, with a new perspective. You see all of life as God sees it and begin to live for eternity, not for earthly things.

—You are *fearfully and wonderfully made*. God reports that you (yes, you!) are one of His "marvelous" works (Psalm 139:14). As I said, true beauty is internal. And the transformations considered here take place on the *inside*. God in you and at work in you causes you to be beautiful in Him on the inside. And, as two well-worn sayings remind us, "Beauty is only skin deep" and "It's what's on the inside that counts." So don't put down the way you look or resent your appearance. Instead remember who you are in Christ.

These assurances from God's Word have been lifesavers for me. So much so that they have eliminated all my concerns about "self"-image. My thinking now goes like this: *If*

God has transformed me from the inside out, caused me to become a new creation, and put His stamp of approval on my appearance, then who am I to find fault with His creation? Whenever I read or remember that I am a new creation and that I am fearfully and wonderfully made (and I can't help but add in my heart "... *exactly* the way I am!"), then I must take the next obvious step and praise God (Psalm 139:14)!

2. *True beauty is enhanced by spiritual growth.* Here's an all-too-familiar fact about our appearance: We learn from 2 Corinthians 4:16 that "our *outward* man is perishing"—the physical body is in the process of decaying, a process that leads finally to physical death. That's the bad news.

The good news is that even as your body is declining, "the *inward* man is being renewed day by day" (also verse 16). In other words, your soul is constantly growing and maturing in Christlikeness as you concentrate on "the things which are *not* seen" rather than with "the things which *are* seen" (verse 18). Being obsessed with that which is *eternal* instead of that which is *earthly* makes a difference...even in your appearance. How?

I'm sure you're familiar with lovely women who exude spiritual strength and beauty. They are flesh-and-blood pictures of the verse at the beginning of this chapter. "Strength and honor" are their "clothing" (Proverbs 31:25). You hardly notice what they look like because you're so caught up in something they convey. There's a definite aura about them. No, there's no halo. But there is an air, a charm, a sparkle, a glow. And somehow you know it comes from within. It's spiritual.

What you're witnessing is a beautiful inner life radiating outward. As one has termed it, it's the "beauty treatment" of godliness and deep spirituality that helps them—and us!—to become truly lovely. It's the beauty of "patience, kindness, and joy" along with "a gentle, modest, loving character [that] gives a light to the face that cannot be duplicated by the best cosmetics and jewelry in the world."[2]

Meet Rebekah

As we first meet Rebekah, she's described by God as "very beautiful to behold" (Genesis 24:16). Yet the servant of Abraham, who was sent to find a wife for Abraham's son Isaac, was attracted to something else in this gorgeous woman. He was drawn to her obvious compassion toward him as a tired man who had trekked hundreds of miles across the burning desert, to her sweet willingness to minister to him by bringing him water, and by her energy as she ran to tote enough water to also refresh his ten camels. You see, Abraham's servant was not looking for a model. He was looking for a *model servant*. And that quality is found only on the inside, in the heart.

That's what we want—inner beauty. And a sure way to encourage spiritual growth and enhance inner beauty is by dipping into God's fountain of beauty—His Word, the Bible—"day by day" (2 Corinthians 4:16). So let the beauty treatment begin!

3. *True beauty is a matter of the heart.* We can't leave our beauty treatment without considering what I call "the queen of truths." Here's how the apostle Peter put it:

> Do not let your adornment be merely outward—arranging the hair, wearing gold, or putting on fine apparel—rather let it be the hidden person of the heart, with the incorruptible beauty of a gentle and quiet spirit, which is very precious in the sight of God (1 Peter 3:3-4).

Peter is not telling us to ignore attempts at a pleasing appearance. He is rather pointing the finger at those who are so obsessed with what's on the outside that they fail to take care of what's on the inside—the inner person of the heart. And how can we take care of the heart? By tending to a gentle and quiet spirit. By concentrating on godly character, which is "precious in the sight of God."

Unfortunately, it's true that "man looks at the outward appearance" (1 Samuel 16:7). This may not be right, and it may not be fair—but it is true. But here's another truth—"The Lord does not see as man sees...the Lord looks at the heart" (also verse 7). So make it a priority to tend to your heart, to your faith, and to your character. This finds favor with God. This is precious in His sight. So whatever amount of time you spend maintaining your physical looks, do even more to cultivate your inner character.

Checklist for Your Heart

We'll get to your actual outward clothing and appearance in the next chapter. But for now we are interested in visiting God's spiritual clothing closet and putting on the apparel that is "very precious in the sight of God" (1 Peter 3:4). Look into the mirror of His Word and check out your heart. How does your adornment match up with God's list for His best-dressed women? Are there any changes that need to be made?

- Put on...the new man (Ephesians 4:24).

- Put on...tender mercies,

- Put on...kindness,

- Put on...humbleness of mind,

- Put on...meekness, and

- Put on...longsuffering (Colossians 3:12).

- Put on...a gentle and quiet spirit (1 Peter 3:4).

- Put on...a cloak of humility (1 Peter 5:5).

Just for Today...

As I said before, many women worry about their appearance or don't like their looks. They fuss and fume over what they consider their lacks and shortcomings in the Beauty Department. If you're one of these women...or you know other women or have daughters who struggle in this area, please follow and share these steps to help them live according to God's plan.

❑   Just for today...take the truths we've gone over in this chapter to heart. Believe it—*You* are God's workmanship. You are a new creation in Christ. You are fearfully and wonderfully made. You are one of God's marvelous works. So just for today follow

David's example. As he thought upon truths like these, he rejoiced, "I will praise You" (Psalm 139:14)! Thank and praise God now!

❏ Just for tomorrow...purpose to repeat the step above if (or when!) you find yourself complaining or displeased with your looks or comparing your appearance with that of someone else, someone you consider to be more beautiful than you. Focus instead on the spiritual realities of who you are in Christ.

Also, just for tomorrow (and all your tomorrows) work on your inner beauty. Look in the mirror of God's Word. Spend time there reading, meditating, praying. Then share your beauty with others. Be kind to as many people as you can. Be gracious. Be sweet. Be loving. Be an encourager. Be patient. Be gentle. Be compassionate. Be helpful. Share your better life with others. It will better their lives too.

That's what Rebekah did as she spotted an elderly, lone, tired, dusty traveler. As she poured out water, the evidence of her heart was obvious in its overflow. True beauty is a gift *from* God and *of* God. As someone wrote regarding Rebekah's beautiful spirit of servanthood, "To be my very best this very hour, to do the very best for those about me, and to spend this moment in a spirit of absolute consecration to God's glory...is in the noblest sense to live for eternity."[3] That's the kind of beauty we want...today, tomorrow, and beyond.

❏ Just for this week...follow God's plan each day. Seek to multiply your one beautiful day times seven. Begin your beautiful strand of beautiful deeds by adding seven beautiful "pearls" to it this week. Dedicate your mind to thinking on what is true about yourself, about your core, about your heart, about what God has done for you (Philippians 4:8). Honor God by refusing to think otherwise. Then a wonderful thing will happen. Due to this one small change, you'll find that the more you think on the truth about your internal beauty, the less you'll think about yourself...and the more you'll think about the Lord and others. What a marvelous day it will be when you don't even think about yourself at all because you're secure in Him and other oriented.

Living God's Plan

For many years, it's been my joy to write extensively on what it means to be "a woman after God's own heart."[4] Such a woman knows that beauty—true beauty—begins in the heart, inside a woman at her very core. Begin praying, "Lord, grant that I may become inwardly beautiful." A woman after God's own heart seeks to be noticed not for her clothing, jewelry, figure, skin tone, or hairdo, but rather for her kind and good character. She follows God's plan for His women of being sensible in manner and noticed for the "good works" that accompany a woman who professes godliness (1 Timothy 2:9-10).

For a better life, take the steps outlined in this chapter. May strength and honor be your clothing. May others say of you, "Strong and beautiful is her clothing of moral character and honorable conduct. She is a true woman of excellence!"

*G*od's *G*uidelines for a *B*etter *L*ife

❧ Always remember you are known and blessed by God—*"Before I formed you in the womb I knew you; before you were born I sanctified you"* (Jeremiah 1:5).

❧ Always remember you are loved by God, and His Son died for your sins—*"God demonstrates His own love toward us, in that while we were still sinners, Christ died for us"* (Romans 5:8).

❧ Always remember you are accepted by God through His Son—*"Blessed be the God and Father of our Lord Jesus Christ, who has blessed us with every spiritual blessing....He chose us in Him before the foundation of the world...having predestined us to adoption as sons...by which He has made us accepted in the Beloved"* (Ephesians 1:3-6).

❧ Always remember you are complete in Christ— *"For in Him dwells all the fullness of the Godhead bodily; and you are complete in Him"* (Colossians 2:9-10).

❧ Always remember you are a work in progress and will one day be perfect!—*"Being confident of this very thing, that He who has begun a good work in you will complete it until the day of Jesus Christ"* (Philippians 1:6).

As we look up to Him, pray to Him, think on Him, serve Him, worship Him, do all unto Him, obey Him, love Him with all our hearts, souls, strength, and minds, it is His beauty that shines through our lowly efforts. And then *He* is glorified!

—E<small>LIZABETH</small> G<small>EORGE</small>

Tend to Your Appearance

*A*s a young teen in junior high school, I was required to take a home economics class on grooming. Now that was a class none of us girls complained about! Oh no! We thrived on learning about the proper way to take care of our skin, apply makeup, groom our nails. We even learned tips on good posture, how to enter a room, how to "sit like a lady," and... On and on the wonderful topics and beauty tips went. We couldn't get enough.

Every woman—whether young or old—is concerned about her appearance. Some, as we learned in the previous chapter, are overly concerned. But as we now know, true beauty is what's inside.

More Timeless Beauty Tips

In the last chapter we began a list of God's timeless beauty tips. We learned that true beauty is internal, true beauty is enhanced by spiritual growth, and true beauty is a matter of the heart. Now let's get more help for tending to our inner beauty!

167

4. *True beauty is also external.* Yes, your appearance is a mirror of what's happening (or not happening!) on the inside. It's an outward reflection of the inner self (1 Peter 3:4). However, you can do a few things, make some small changes, and take a few steps to maintain and improve your external appearance. What are God's guidelines and what is His dress code?

Modesty—The Bible says to adorn yourself "in modest apparel" (1 Timothy 2:9). This means wearing decent clothing that reveals a properly adorned chaste heart.[1] As one scholar comments, "respectable and honorable apparel reflects a godly woman's inner life."[2] Modesty exhibits a right attitude of mind because what a woman wears is, again, a mirror of her mind and heart. God desires His women to be "chaste" (Titus 2:5). Therefore your appearance should be modest, showing forth a chaste and pure heart.

As I thought about modesty, I went to a dictionary for help. There I found that *modesty* is also defined simply as a lack of excesses or pretensions. Modesty is wrapped up in moderation and in decency mixed with decorum. So to be modest is to behave, dress, and speak in a way that is considered proper...especially before God.

Propriety—The Bible says to "adorn" yourself with all "propriety" or reverence (1 Timothy 2:9). *Propriety* refers to modesty mixed with humility.[3] Clearly this is a tall order! I can never think about this call to propriety and reverence in clothing without thinking of Proverbs 31:30 (NASB): "Charm is deceitful and beauty is vain, but a woman who fears the LORD, she shall be praised."

Moderation—The Bible says to adorn yourself with moderation, with a serious air of self-restraint, "not with braided hair or gold or pearls or costly clothing" (1 Timothy 2:9). In the day of Paul and Timothy, women wore their wealth. They tended to dress excessively. For them, the "more" you saw revealed the "more" they possessed. Paul says not so for the woman who is centered on holiness.

Dressing with *moderation* (1 Timothy 2:9) also refers to self-control "so as not to lead another into sin."[4] By contrast, the prostitute in Proverbs 7:10 wore "the attire of a harlot" or, in the words of another, she was "dressed to kill."[5]

I like what my former pastor, Dr. John MacArthur, wrote in his commentary on the appearance we are to desire:

What's a Woman to Wear?

How does a woman discern the sometimes fine line between proper dress and dressing to be the center of attention? The answer starts in the intent of the heart. A woman should examine her motives and goals for the way she dresses. Is her intent to show the grace and beauty of womanhood? Is it to show her love and devotion to her husband and his goodness to her? Is it to reveal a humble heart devoted to worshiping God? Or is it to call attention to herself, and flaunt her wealth and beauty? Or worse, to attempt to allure men sexually? A woman who focuses on worshiping God will consider carefully how she is dressed, because her heart will dictate her wardrobe and appearance.[6]

So what's a woman to wear? The next time you look in your mirror, check yourself out...

>...for modesty—"Do I look pure?"

>...for propriety—"Is my appearance reflecting a proper image of a woman of God?"

>...for moderation—"Would my appearance cause someone to stumble?"

And here's another test. We're not to adorn ourselves with too much (1 Timothy 2:9). So ask yourself the "too much" question—Am I wearing too much? Too much makeup? Too much jewelry? Are my clothes too fancy? Too gaudy? Am I wearing items that would cause others to notice me and my clothing, hair, or jewelry, rather than my godliness and good works (verse 10)?

Practical Beauty Tips

It truly is what's on the inside that counts with God. But there are practical steps we can take to represent Christ well. Then what others see in us will honor Him (Titus 2:5).

Dress up—The Old Testament heroine Queen Esther chose to wear her royal robes into the presence of her husband, the king (Esther 5:1). The Proverbs 31 woman wore silk and purple (Proverbs 31:22 KJV). Each of these women dressed with a touch of class, wearing what was right for the occasion and proper in her day and time.

For years I've taught the following principles about "dressing up" to women in Christian leadership and pastors' wives:

Become a role model for your peers and those you want to lead. And always model yourself after people you respect. Don't model yourself after the group in which you run....Be different if it means being cleaner, neater, and better groomed than the group. It is always better to arrive at any function looking slightly better than others rather than slightly worse than the others.[7]

Why not bless others with a pleasing appearance? They will be most grateful! And you will be setting a good example.

Fix up—Make it a daily step to create a pleasing appearance. When I'm getting ready in the morning, I always think about my husband and about the fact that he has to look at me. What is he seeing? Something fresh (as in a freshly washed face, freshly fixed hair, and fresh makeup)? Something clean (as in wrinkle-free, spot-free, odor-free clothes)? Something bright (as in a bright smile, a little color here and there)? Even when my children were still living at home, I was always concerned that they be able to look at me, rather than needing to avert their eyes because of what I looked like. I wanted them to be proud of me when I picked them up from school or took them to a friend's house, piano lessons, or their church group.

So fix up...a little. Make up...a little. Dress up...a little. Shape up...a little.

Clean up—We've all heard the adage that cleanliness is next to godliness. Plus Proverbs teaches us that "ointment and perfume delight the heart" (27:9). Both are pleasant and heartwarming and indicate someone has gone to the trouble to spruce up.

Look up—Back to the Lord we go. As we look up to Him, pray to Him, think on Him, serve Him, worship Him, do all unto Him, obey Him, love Him with all our hearts, souls, strength, and minds (Luke 10:27), and are consciously aware of His presence, it is His beauty that shines through our efforts. And then *He* is glorified (Matthew 5:16)!

Just for Today...

One of the things I learned from my home economics class on basic grooming is that good grooming means daily grooming. That's how teeth are tended to, skin is cared for, hair is maintained, and nails are kept up. So when it comes to your physical appearance...

❏ Just for today...follow these four steps: Fix up...a little. Make up...a little. Dress up...a little. Shape up...a little. Think about your family members and the people you see every day. Think of your efforts as blessing them, as giving them a gift.

And here's another thought: Think about the Lord as you prepare to represent Him to the world. What impressions do you give to others about what Christians and Christianity are? When you take care of your appearance, God is represented in a good light.

❏ Just for tomorrow...remember, good grooming is done daily. So tomorrow set aside a small pocket of time, such as 10 to 20 minutes, to take care of your appearance. Most women love the "makeover" shows on television. The premise behind these makeovers is that if a woman will spend just 20 minutes each morning on her looks, it will set her apart from others (in a good way). We're not talking about wowing others. We're just talking about looking nice, pleasant, attractive—a habitat of the Spirit of Christ who lives within you.

❏ Just for this week…imagine (speaking of makeovers) what one week of paying attention to your appearance will mean. If you think personal hygiene takes too long and you're already too busy, take heart. As you repeat your efforts, you'll get faster. You'll become more organized and streamlined as you develop a quick and simple daily routine of taking care of yourself.

And here's another piece of advice an "older woman" gave me. Put a Scripture memory verse in your bathroom or on your makeup table. Then as you tend to the "outward man" (2 Corinthians 4:16), you will also be adorning "the hidden person of the heart" (1 Peter 3:4). After all, all things are to be done for the Lord (Colossians 3:23).

Living God's Plan

Think about it—your appearance is a daily thing. And every day you must go to your closets. You must fling open the doors, peer inside, think through your day, and select the clothes you put on. While you're not responsible for how you were born, for your physical genetics and features, you are responsible for what you choose to wear and not wear, for the message you choose to send through your dress and grooming.

What message do you wish to send? Now that you've thought about God's standards, make the changes that will send a loud and clear message that you belong to God. That you've put God at the center of your life. That you are truly "all about God." Then "adorn" (meaning arrange, make ready, and put in order) yourself properly and prayerfully for Him, in a way that honors Him and speaks well of Him. Choose the purposeful, orderly, and proper arrangement of your appearance as a daily habit of life. Dress to impress God, to catch the look of approval in His eyes, to draw attention to your godliness and good works so that your Father who is in heaven is glorified (Matthew 5:16). It's a small change—but one that sends a big message.

God's Guidelines for a Better Life

❧ Develop godly character—it is your best outfit!—*"Strength and honor are her clothing"* (Proverbs 31:25).

❧ Seek God's approval rather than that of the world—*"Charm is deceitful and beauty is passing, but a woman who fears the LORD, she shall be praised"* (Proverbs 31:30).

❧ Watch what you wear—your clothing is sending a message!—*"And there a woman met him, with the attire of a harlot, and a crafty heart. She was loud and rebellious"* (Proverbs 7:10-11).

❧ Wear what is appropriate for the occasion and as a daughter of the King—*"In like manner also, that the women adorn themselves in modest apparel, with propriety and moderation, not with braided hair or gold or pearls or costly clothing, but, which is proper for women professing godliness, with good works"* (1 Timothy 2:9-10).

❧ Don't worry about following the crowd—you have a higher standard—*"Beloved, do not imitate what is evil, but what is good"* (3 John 11).

Discipline is evident on every page of the life of
Daniel….The first thing that sets Daniel apart from…
others is his decision [about what] not to eat….It was the
beginning of the Lord's preparation of a man whose
spiritual fiber would be rigorously tested later on.[1]

—ELISABETH ELLIOT

Are there things you desire to accomplish, goals you'd
like to achieve, dreams you'd like to see come true—
a better life? Then follow God's plan in the area of food.
Doing so will bring the much-needed energy to your life.

—ELIZABETH GEORGE

Watch What You Eat

*Y*ou are what you eat." Heard this saying before? I've also heard arguments on whether this statement is true or not. But I'm sure you agree that what you take in and feed on—whether physically, mentally, or visually—has a powerful effect on the quality of your daily life. It can also influence the direction your life takes. But let's focus for now on the physical appetite, on what we eat. Let's see what changes need to be made for a better life.

I still remember (all too well!) a phase in my life when I tried to gain the energy I needed as a young wife and mother of preschoolers by drinking colas and eating candy, cookies, and (I confess) even the cookie dough. And I also remember the glucose-drinking and blood work required by a doctor that revealed I was taking in too much sugar—more than my body could process. No wonder I was sluggish, drowsy, and needed a nap every day after lunch! For me the statement was true—I was what I was eating! I was a junk food addict.

After this ordeal, believe me, I wanted to know what God had to say on the subject of food. After all, I was seeking to live for Him and to live out His plan for me. I dearly wanted a better life, one that included energy and a clear head. It was obvious that the plan I was following was not a good one. I was on the wrong track, a track that was leading to an unhealthy lifestyle and sabotaging my dreams of a life of get-up-and-go, order, and achievement. I was looking in the wrong places for the energy I wanted and needed as a busy woman.

So back to the Bible I went, looking for God's guidelines on this daily issue of diet. And of course there it was...right in my Bible—God's guidance regarding what to eat and not eat.

Do you want more energy? Or should I say, Do you *need* more energy? Are there things you want to accomplish, goals you'd like to achieve, dreams you'd like to see come true— such as a better life? Then make a few small changes in your eating habits. Follow God's plan in the area of food. Doing so will bring the much-needed energy to your life...because His way works.

Better Eating God's Way!

One scripture puts a completely spiritual spin on our eating habits: "Therefore, whether you eat or drink, or whatever you do, do all to the glory of God" (1 Corinthians 10:31). This truth says it's possible for us to eat in a way that glorifies and honors the Lord. Just think about that for a second. We give glory to God in the everyday way we eat and drink when we follow a few of God's steps for better eating and better living.

Rule 1—Do not eat too much. Why? One reason is obvious. We feel terrible when we've eaten in excess! We actually feel sick. The Bible puts this feeling in very graphic terms—"Have you found honey? Eat only as much as you need, lest you be filled with it and vomit" (Proverbs 25:16). Now that's vivid!

But there are two other reasons in the Bible for not eating too much. One I had already experienced...and the other was a surprise, something I hadn't thought about before. According to Proverbs, eating too much (referred to as "gluttony") *costs too much* and *causes us to sleep too much*. As Solomon put it, "The drunkard and the glutton will come to poverty, and drowsiness will clothe a man with rags" (Proverbs 23:21). In other words, "There are two kinds of drunkards—those who drink too much and those who eat too much."[2]

What are some other costs to overeating?

The physical—I already knew (from firsthand experience!) about the sleepy effect of overeating. Drowsiness, laziness, and dullness are sure results from overeating and from eating the wrong kinds of food. I already knew about living in a daze. And here I was reading in the Bible that those who overindulge in food will suffer physically. They'll live in a fog, a tired state, and a sort of drunken stupor. As a result they'll lack the energy and clearheadedness needed to do their work and manage lives that are busy and filled to the brim with responsibilities (Proverbs 23:20-21).

The financial—But here was the surprise for me—not only will one who overeats pay a price physically, but she'll also pay a price financially. She'll suffer from a lack of funds. As one scholar so succinctly dubbed this passage of Scripture, the unwise ones go "from Revelry to Rags"![3] We can almost imagine self-conversations like this: *Wow, it was fun while it lasted...but, boy oh boy, was there a price to pay later!*

If you think about it, where does most of the food a woman eats come from? It comes from her efforts. She shops for it. She purchases it. She pays for it, maybe even earning the money herself for it. She brings it home. Whether at a restaurant or a grocery store or a food warehouse, each woman puts out money for the food she puts into her mouth and into her pantry.

Here's an exercise—Think of all you desire for yourself and for your family that involves finances. And think of all the people and concerns you could bless with your money. For instance, Do you want to get out of debt? Do you want to save for your children's or grandchildren's college years? Do you want to send your teen to the church's youth retreat? Do you desire to contribute to a worthy ministry or relief cause? Do you want to pay off your home mortgage early? Maybe even take a much-needed vacation? Then you must think twice—and pray!—before you go out to eat or run to the food store. Money not spent on eating too much (or eating out too much, or stocking your cupboards with too much junk food) is money in the bank, money for better things than the sensual indulgence of overeating.

The spiritual—As I continued my research (frankly not liking what I was reading!), I found another principle for better living, a principle in the area of spiritual life. One commentator put it this way—"Bad habits grow together."[4] The implication is that overeating goes against the wisdom and teaching of God's Word, which leads to a life of guilt, which leads to a seared conscience, which leads to a deadening of the heart to spiritual truth. In other words, overeating has far greater consequences than merely gaining weight. It affects your spiritual life!

The practical—And what about your time and your life? Quite simply, the glutton's "time is divided between eating ...and sleeping."[5] This misuse of time and life is the practical effect of a failure to manage your food intake God's way.

A prayer for a better life...

> Lord, may a lifestyle of physical fatigue, financial folly, spiritual deadening, and the misuse of time not be true of me! Help me live my life in a better way—in Your way. Amen.

Just for Today...

Unfortunately, we learn more from failure than from success. And frankly I know many women who have failed in this area of food and are waging an active battle against their eating habits. They're making the changes that lead to a better life. They're taking the daily steps to live out God's principles regarding food choices. I'm in their camp, and I heartily applaud them. It's also true that habit is either the worst of masters or the best of servants. And bad habits reap failure for us in the Food Department.

So now we must begin...just for today...to break the cords of harmful habits and replace them with a chain of good habits so God's strong spiritual disciplines become the best of servants for us.

❏   Just for today...write out, memorize, and carry with
you 1 Corinthians 10:31—"Therefore, whether you
eat or drink, or whatever you do, do all to the glory
of God." Make this the rule of your eating and
drinking habits...just for today. Also pray this *Prayer
for a Better Life,* which I am repeating here. Pray it
now and each time you prepare to eat.

> Lord, may a lifestyle of physical fatigue, financial
> folly, spiritual deadening, and the misuse of time
> not be true of me! Help me live my life in a better
> way—in Your way.

❏   Just for tomorrow...begin following the steps in this
checklist.
#1—*Do not eat too much.*

- Eat only when you are hungry.
- Eat only after you pray.
- Eat only one helping.
- Eat half-portions.
- Eat on a small plate.
- Eat on a schedule.
- Eat what is healthy.
- Eat what will give you energy.
- Eat to the glory of God.

❏   Just for this week...keep records of your eating
habits. I've learned the habit of journaling, and I
recommend the same for you. Just for this week,
daily write out 1 Corinthians 10:31 in a journal or a
notebook. At the beginning of each day, write down

your weight. Throughout each day, write down everything you eat and the exact time you eat it. Go a step further and record how you felt physically and mentally after you ate. Pay attention to what foods eaten in what quantities at what times put you down or picked you up in the Energy Department. Then you can make changes each day toward a better life. These changes will help you become the vibrant woman you want to be.

Living God's Plan

Wisdom is "the ability to see with discernment....to view life as God perceives it."[6] And, dear reader, God has spoken on our eating habits. He's given us His view and His instruction. In short, He says, *Do not eat too much*. Now the question is, Will you heed His truths? Will you make the changes necessary? Will you follow God's plan for your health and nutrition? Will you make His principle your own? A better life is waiting for your *"Yes!"*

God's Guidelines for a Better Life

- Do everything to the glory of God, including what and how you eat—*"Whatever you do in word or deed, do all in the name of the Lord Jesus, giving thanks to God the Father through Him"* (Colossians 3:17).

- Eat only what betters your life—*"All things are lawful for me, but all things are not helpful. All things are lawful for me, but I will not be brought under the power of any"* (1 Corinthians 6:12).

- Restrain yourself! Don't stuff yourself!—*"When you sit down to eat with a ruler, consider carefully what is before you; and put a knife to your throat[7] if you are a man given to appetite"* (Proverbs 23:1-2).

- Don't let inactivity rob your strength—*"A lazy man buries his hand in the bowl, and will not so much as bring it to his mouth again"* (Proverbs 19:24).

- Look to Christ for His help while avoiding tempting situations—*"Put on the Lord Jesus Christ, and make no provision for the flesh, to fulfill its lusts"* (Romans 13:14).

Let us not be Christians as to the few great things of our lives, and atheists as to the many small things which fill up a far greater space of them. God is in both, waiting for the glory we can give Him in them.[1]

—DWIGHT L. MOODY

Eat Just Enough

*M*y daughter Courtney is a wonderful amateur chef. She's always trying to improve and add new skills and recipes to her mastery. She's even spent time in the classrooms of a famous Colorado cooking institute. So quite naturally Courtney's coffee table at home is spread with the cooking magazines she subscribes to. One of these publications is *Bon Appétit*…which translates into English as "good appetite" or "enjoy your meal."

Unfortunately, many of us enjoy our good and enjoyable eating a little too much! That's why we're looking to God for His guidelines in the Eating Department. So far we've learned *Rule 1—Do not eat too much*. Now…

More on Better Eating God's Way!

Rule 2—Do eat only what is sufficient. I love this prayer from the Bible—"Feed me with the food allotted to me; lest I be full and deny You" (Proverbs 30:8-9). Other translations explain this to mean "feed me with the food that is *needful* and *sufficient* for me, *just enough* to satisfy my needs."[2] One scholar actually put the prayer in these fairly familiar words—"Give me only *my daily bread*"—pointing out a distinction between human wants and human needs.[3]

And why is eating only what is sufficient so important? So we are not tempted to forget, deny, or become independent of God because we've overindulged. So we don't fail to trust in the Lord as our Provider. Obviously the extremes of too much or too little affect our character. Those who have too much (and eat too much) are puffed up by the pride of prosperity, and those who have too little are tempted to assault God's mercy, righteousness, and justice.

Thus God's answer is that we eat "just enough."

Rule 3—Do eat only what you need. This may sound like a repeat of Rule 2. But it contains an additional flavor, if you will. Instead of overindulging, God calls us to eat only as much as we need (Proverbs 25:16). To keep us from sin, God says we are simply to eat what is enough. In other words, eat to live—don't live to eat.

Rule 4—Do not be mastered by anything. And note—"anything" includes food. In the New Testament we read: "All things are lawful for me, but all things are not helpful. All things are lawful for me, but I will not be brought under the power of any" (1 Corinthians 6:12). Generally speaking, Paul is saying that not everything a Christian *could* do is helpful or beneficial or profitable or useful. Therefore, don't do them!

To top off his instruction, Paul adds the argument of enslavement, declaring, "I will not be brought under the power of any." In other words, Paul is putting his foot down and refusing to become enslaved to or brought under the power of *anything*. Regardless of what *others may do,* and regardless of what *he could do,* Paul will not follow the crowd. He simply will not become a slave! Paul plays with the words of this principle:

> *All things* are in my *power,* but I will not be brought under the *power* of any of the *all* things.[4]

We know sin is powerful and enslaving. Nevertheless, for a better life, we "must never allow sin to have…control, but must master it in the Lord's strength."[5] God can help us to master anything, even our appetite for food.

Rule 5—Do eat in a way that glorifies God. This is God's final word on all our behavior, including our eating—"Therefore, whether you eat or drink, or whatever you do, do all to the glory of God" (1 Corinthians 10:31). This means that even the most common acts of eating and drinking can be done in a way that honors our Lord. Imagine! We can actually eat in a way that brings honor and glory to God! So give God glory and honor Him *when* you eat, by *what* you eat, and *how* you eat. And a major side benefit will be thrown in as you follow this scriptural command—the caliber of your life, as well as your worship, will improve. That means…a better life!

Just for Today…

Hopefully by now your chain of good habits—habits that make for a better life—especially in this area of the very food you put into your mouth, is lengthening and strengthening. And hopefully by now you're realizing that your chain of good habits is created one habit at a time, one choice at a time, one day at a time, and one week at a time. So...

❏ Just for today...seek to comprehend these rules from God's Word:

Rule 1—Do not eat too much.

Rule 2—Do eat only what is sufficient.

Rule 3—Do eat only what you need.

Rule 4—Do not be mastered by anything.

Rule 5—Do eat in a way that glorifies God.

Look again at each rule. Pinpoint the one that needs the most attention. What will you do about it? What will you change...just for today? Habit is overcome by habit. That means old habits are overcome by new habits. Bad habits are overcome by good habits. So what new habit will you begin to groom to replace and overcome the one you selected, a habit that is keeping you from a better life, a habit that is interfering with living God's plan?

❏ Just for tomorrow...look again at the checklist from the previous chapter (on page 182) for eating "just enough." Add these to the checklist:

• Eat with God in mind.

• Eat to live instead of living to eat.

• Eat for health.

• Eat for energy.

• Eat with self-mastery.

- Eat as a Christian, not as an atheist.

❑ Just for this week...purpose, with God's help, to make it through one day at a time for one week. Imagine! If one day of God-honoring, God-glorifying eating practices is a golden link in your chain of good habits, a week is an outstanding beginning, a giant step toward a better life! Purpose to add a link a day...for life.

Living God's Plan

Honestly, I have to admit that I dislike writing on this subject. Why? Because I don't want to sound legalistic or like I have my act together in this area. Plus I know it's a difficult area for most women to stomach. We simply don't want to hear about sensible eating (again!) and self-control (again!). And we don't want to have to think about them (again!). And we certainly dislike dealing with them (again!).

But at the same time, I do want to live my life by God's plan. And I do want a better life! There are so many things I passionately long to do in my life and with my life and for the others in my life. Believe me, there is an urgency to live out God's will that arrives with each new sunrise. And I've decided that I don't want the remaining years, months, weeks, days, hours, and minutes of my life (and only God knows how many are left) to be spent in a fog with a headache and a tired, overindulged body that can't pull off the desires of my heart. I just can't afford it! And I don't think you can either.

So although it is hard to do, I do want to share the wisdom I've found in the Bible with you and the many, many other women who write to me or share their personal battles with weight gain and numerous eating disorders with me. I know what a challenge managing the appetite is. But I also know that it's an assignment from God. God calls us to self-control (Galatians 5:23), to moderation (1 Timothy 2:9), to temperance (1 Timothy 3:11), to walk worthily (Ephesians 4:1), to walk in wisdom (Colossians 4:5), and to receive and treasure His timeless principles (Proverbs 2:1-2), even in the area of the food we choose to put into our mouths.

As we finish up this issue of appetite, food, and eating habits, I think you'll find the story that follows to be absolutely delightful. It's a fitting—and fun—illustration of many of the guidelines and steps we've learned in this important area of our lives.

Enjoy! *Bon appétit!*

Too Much of a Good Thing

Some friends of ours have eight children, and they all love ice cream. On a hot summer day, one of the younger ones declared that she wished they could eat nothing but ice cream. The others chimed agreement, and to their surprise the father said, "All right. Tomorrow you can have all the ice cream you want—nothing but ice cream!" The children squealed with delight and could hardly contain themselves until the next day. They came trooping down to breakfast shouting their orders for choco-late, strawberry, or vanilla ice cream—soup bowls full! Mid-morning snack—ice cream again. Lunch—ice cream, this time slightly smaller portions. When they came in for mid-afternoon snack, their mother was just taking some fresh muffins out of the oven, and the aroma wafted through the whole house.

"Oh goody!" said little Teddy. "Fresh muffins—my favorite!" He made a move for the jam cup-board, but his mother stopped him.

"Don't you remember? It's ice cream day—nothing but ice cream."

"Oh yeah..."

"Want to sit up for a bowl?"

"No thanks. Just give me a one-dip cone."

By suppertime the enthusiasm for an all-ice cream diet had waned considerably. As they sat staring at fresh bowls of ice cream, Mary—whose suggestion had started this whole adventure—looked up at her daddy and said, "Couldn't we just trade in this ice cream for a crust of bread?"[6]

God's Guidelines for
a Better Life

⚜ Correct your perspective on what is really important—*"For the kingdom of God is not eating and drinking, but righteousness and peace and joy in the Holy Spirit"* (Romans 14:17).

⚜ Your body belongs to the Lord, therefore don't violate His standards for it—*"Do you not know that your body is the temple of the Holy Spirit...? Therefore glorify God in your body"* (1 Corinthians 6:19-20).

⚜ Edify yourself, not gratify yourself!—*"All things are lawful for me, but all things are not helpful; all things are lawful for me, but not all things edify"* (1 Corinthians 10:23).

⚜ Always ask, Is my eating glorifying God, or how can I honor God through my eating? *"Therefore, whether you eat or drink, or whatever you do, do all to the glory of God"* (1 Corinthians 10:31).

⚜ Bite by bite give God control of your food intake and appetite—*"But the fruit of the Spirit is...self-control"* (Galatians 5:22-23).

The person who does not avoid small faults, little by little slips into greater ones. You will always be glad at evening if you have spent the day well. Watch over yourself, rouse yourself, chide yourself, and no matter what others may do, do not neglect yourself.[1]

—Thomas à Kempis

The more self-disciplined you are,
the more you will progress.[2]

—Thomas à Kempis

Grow in Discipline

I admit that I need help with discipline…every day of my life! From my first decision each morning in answer to the sound of my alarm clock (Will I respond or not? Will I get up or snooze in?) to the final decision at day's end of putting my head on my pillow (Will I read a little longer, work a little longer, watch television a little longer, or will I turn out the light and get to sleep so I can get up when the alarm goes off?), I need discipline.

No one has to tell you or me that discipline in every area of life is crucial. You already know that discipline is important for what it produces in you—spiritual growth, personal accomplishment, and physical well-being…in other words, a better life. But discipline is also important for what it produces in you that is seen by others, which in turn can produce change in them. You can be a motivating model and an example. And whether you like it or not, others are watching you. Your life has a positive or negative effect on everyone you live with, know, or encounter.

And yet, no matter how disciplined (or undisciplined!) you already are, there's always room for growth. There's always another area you can tackle and improve. There's always something to learn, try, and perfect...a small change to make or a new step to take. So let's rethink this vital ingredient in life. Exactly why is a disciplined life so critical? And most important, what does God have to say about discipline?

God's Take on Discipline

Recognize that discipline is a spiritual issue—Self-control and self-discipline are manifestations of God's Spirit at work in us (Galatians 5:22-23). The Bible says that if we are walking by the Spirit (verse 16)—if we're seeking to live our lives according to His plan—we will exhibit self-control. This word literally means to be master of one's self. Picture wrapping your arms around yourself and grasping onto yourself and holding yourself in restraint. That's self-control. Try that the next time you have a desire to overindulge in some area. And remember...character does not reach its best until it is controlled, harnessed, and disciplined.

Readily acknowledge sin—It helps to understand that self-control is energized by the power of the Holy Spirit in you. As you walk by the Spirit, He gives you the ability to overcome the temptations of the flesh (Galatians 5:16). But sin and disobedience grieve the Holy Spirit of God and quench the Spirit and His power to help you in your fight against sin (Ephesians 4:30 and 1 Thessalonians 5:19). So if you want to experience self-discipline, you must keep a short account with God. Quickly confess your sins—any of them and all of them. The result of this one step is a victorious life of Christian discipline, a life of power and beauty, a better life.

Realize that discipline is an act of the will—Yes, self-control is a fruit of the Spirit, but God's Spirit will not force you to live spiritually. No, you must decide if you will or won't obey the Spirit's promptings in your life. The Holy Spirit doesn't lock your jaw every time you sit down to eat. And He doesn't automatically seal your mouth so you don't yell at your children. The Spirit of God prompts, moves, impresses, and convicts you of error (John 16:8), but He will not force you to live a godly life. Instead He gently leads you as you read, study, pray, and seek to apply God's Word to every area of your life.

Here are a few issues in your life where God's self-control and discipline are needed...and available:

> Your temper—*"Whoever has no rule over his own spirit is like a city broken down, without walls"* (Proverbs 25:28).
>
> Your mouth—*"Even a fool is counted wise when he holds his peace; when he shuts his lips, he is considered perceptive"* (Proverbs 17:28).
>
> Your eating—*"Put a knife to your throat if you are a man given to appetite"* (Proverbs 23:2).
>
> Your diligence—*"Do not love sleep, lest you come to poverty; open your eyes, and you will be satisfied with bread"* (Proverbs 20:13).

In each of these problem areas (as in all others) you have to decide how you're going to respond to that issue in your life. God's Spirit lives in you as a believer in Christ and is ready, willing, and able to assist you with your discipline.

Rejoice with each victory—The battle of the flesh is an ongoing and relentless one. However, as you recognize that self-control is a spiritual issue, realize when and where self-control is needed, and acknowledge your sin, God works in marvelous ways to bring about victory. You *can* live a disciplined life. You *can* have self-control. You *can* manifest God's fruit of self-control as you follow Him. So celebrate each win in your battle against temptation. Rejoice and proclaim, "But thanks be to God, who gives us the victory through our Lord Jesus Christ" (1 Corinthians 15:57). Thank God that there can be victory. And thank God for each and every victory, no matter how great or how small. Each victory is a stairstep toward a disciplined life...which is a better life—a much better one!

Remember that discipline mirrors maturity—As you're able to win (with God's help) the victories of self-control—one issue and one area at a time—an amazing thing happens. You grow spiritually. As you exercise discipline and self-control in any area, your spiritual muscles begin to take shape and are strengthened and developed. You are then better able to handle that area the next time it comes along. It's as one gentleman observed—"No life ever grows great until it is focused, dedicated, and disciplined."[3]

But a word of caution...growth in personal discipline and self-control is not static. You must constantly be about the process of exercising self-control. So stay on your toes!

A Better Life Requires Discipline

Speaking of staying on your toes, whenever I think of discipline—and the lack thereof!—my mind runs simultaneously to two women in the Bible. One gives us a negative example of self-mastery and control and the other a positive one. One was lax and spiritually lazy, and the other stayed on top of things. With which woman do you identify?

Meet Eve

Eve was the first woman on earth and the first woman to fail in the Discipline Department. When it came to the temptation to sin, she was weak, willful, and wanted too much (see Genesis 3). When the serpent began to interact with Eve, she readily entered into a dialog with the master deceiver, "a liar and the father of lies" (John 8:44 NASB). Eve basically...

...wanted too much,

...ate what was forbidden,

...talked too much, and

...held back too little.

Eve chose to disobey God's specific instructions. She also failed to seek counsel, to wait, to weigh her options, and to trust God. Instead Eve jabbered on and on with the devil himself. She doubted God's wisdom, slipped into discontent, questioned God's goodness, lusted for more, ate the forbidden fruit, and also caused her husband to do the same.

Rather than live out God's plan for her life, Eve rushed headlong into sin on every front. Rather than being wise, Eve was a fool. She lived out this bit of biblical wisdom—"He who trusts in his own heart is a fool, but whoever walks wisely will be delivered" (Proverbs 28:26). Her foolish, sinful, selfish, and willful act plunged mankind forever into a fallen state.

Now Meet Abigail...Again

What an amazing woman—so amazing that we're looking at her character again! Abigail was a woman who did things right and models discipline and self-control for us. At a time when everyone around her was out of control, Abigail was quickly and quietly making sure everything was under control. In the biblical account of this woman's life, we see her responding with great wisdom and self-control when her husband made a foolish decision that endangered many lives. Abigail acted with soundness of mind and self-control, stepped into the line of fire, defused the anger of the warrior David, and diverted a life-threatening situation and a potential bloodbath (see 1 Samuel 25). Abigail saved the day and the lives of all!

In this book we're looking at the better life God has in mind for us and the steps that will lead us to it. And do we ever need help in the areas of self-control and discipline! Eve needed it, Abigail needed it, you need it, and so do I. In every area of life God means for us to exercise discipline, moderation, and self-control. That's because discipline and wisdom are essential for a better life.

Just for Today...

How do we become more disciplined? One day at a time. And how do we live out God's plan and move toward a better life? By practicing God's guidelines one day at a time, one act at a time. Now for that one day at a time...

❑ Just for today...pray for God's help in recognizing and avoiding your "little" faults for this day only. Your goal is to live out God's plan. If your little faults aren't avoided or dealt with today, you can be sure they will grow in power and be harder to deal with tomorrow. Long lasting change begins with the tiniest increment of one decision made consistently day after day. So focus your attention...just for today...on one habit, weakness, excuse, or area of neglect. Look to the Lord for His strength. Discipline yourself to forsake your "little" faults. And don't forget to thank God for each "little" victory. Believe me, little steps and small changes will add up to much!

❑ Just for tomorrow...plan your day and pinpoint areas that need improvement. For instance, which area of your life needs God's help and control today? Name it...and then go to the Bible for verses that will help you overcome that area of neglect. Write the verses in your journal or notebook, or at least on 3" x 5" cards to carry with you. Also ask a friend to hold you accountable in the areas that need God's self-control. No victory is won without a battle. And your scriptures, journal, and account-ability partner, coupled with your desire and the power of God's grace, are the weapons of your war-fare. So use your arsenal! Gain the victory! Move toward a better life.

❏ Just for this week...evaluate your growth and changes. A week is a long time...time enough to see marked progress. Time enough to notice mea-surable change. Time enough to "put away" what is wrong and harmful and replace it with more disci-plined choices and conduct. Major progress and inroads can be made in a week of your life. Did you use the help presented in the verses you chose? Did you follow through on your accountability? Did you make any changes, even small ones? Rejoice in any progress and small steps made. Then, without neglecting your new discipline, choose the next area and begin the growth process all over again. Also realize that any progress is for today only. Tomorrow and next week will require fresh com-mitments and new dependence upon the enabling power of the Holy Spirit.

Living God's Plan

Does not wisdom cry out, and understanding lift up her voice? She takes her stand on the top of the high hill, beside the way, where the paths meet. She cries out by the gates, at the entry of the city (Proverbs 8:1-3).

Would you like to be living God's plan? Would you like to stand in places of influence (places like your own home and community) and give godly wisdom to all who care to listen? Then you must embrace discipline as an essential and necessary element in your growth. You cannot lead others—your children, your sisters-in-Christ, your friends, neighbors, and workmates—down a path of righteousness and discipline that you have not personally taken. Only as you exercise self-control will your life be a model for others to follow. With self-control as a guiding principle, you too will be able to "cry out" and "lift up your voice." Others are watching your discipline and listening to your "voice." They are learning from you about a better life. And they are glorifying God for you, for your life of discipline, and for your example. So keep standing on that high hill for all to see and hear! Continue to grow in discipline, and you will continue to stand in the places of influence.

*G*od's *G*uidelines for a *B*etter *L*ife

❧ In all your achievements, don't fail to conquer yourself—*"He who is slow to anger is better than the mighty, and he who rules his spirit than he who takes a city"* (Proverbs 16:32).

❧ Control your mouth, and you control your life— *"Whoever guards his mouth and tongue keeps his soul from troubles"* (Proverbs 21:23).

❧ Realize a contented heart is the soil for growing a disciplined life—*"Give me neither poverty nor riches—feed me with the food allotted to me"* (Proverbs 30:8).

❧ Give maximum effort daily to obtain greater discipline—*"Giving all diligence, add to your faith virtue, to virtue knowledge, to knowledge self-control"* (2 Peter 1:5-6).

❧ Understand that a life of discipline validates your message of Christ—*"I discipline my body and bring it into subjection, lest, when I have preached to others, I myself should become disqualified"* (1 Corinthians 9:27).

Resolutions for Life by
Jonathan Edwards

Live with all my might while I do live.
(He died at age 55.)

Never lose one moment of time,
but improve it in the most profitable way possible.

Work with Diligence

*W*e've covered a lot, haven't we? We've explored life—spiritual life, daily life, family life, and personal life. Obviously we haven't addressed every area of life, but we've certainly considered some of the major ones. And I can think of no better way to end our book than with some words on diligence.

Let me tell you a story...

One of my junior high schoolteachers still stands out as my all-time favorite educator. That's because Miss Spencer used so many creative methods for teaching math. One was a game she called "separating the sheep from the goats." Everyone began Miss Spencer's game by standing. Then, as the math drill progressed, each right answer allowed you to remain standing while one wrong answer meant you had to sit down. In the end, only the "sheep" were standing. The "goats" had been separated out.

Well, my dear friend-on-the-path-to-a-better-life, diligence is a necessary quality for a better life, for perseverance truly separates the sheep from the goats in real life.

Or, as an almost everyday example from my own life illustrates, diligence separates the "be's" from the "wanna-be's." Here's what happens. Just about every day I receive a letter, email, or phone call from someone who says, "I've always wanted to write a book. What advice can you give me?"

And my answer is always the same: "Write the book!" There are many steps that go into getting a book published. But the first step and the main step and the ultimate step is (always has been and always will be)...write the book! Until a book is written, that book is only a dream.

And what does it take to write a book...have an orderly house...get organized...graduate from college...find a job... provide clean clothes for your family...put meals on the table...study the Bible...keep your weight down and your body fit...homeschool your children...be a loving wife...serve in your church...put together a lesson to share some good things with someone else...or to do anything that is worthwhile?

It takes diligence—staying with something until it's finished. It takes work. It takes action. And it takes work, action, and staying with something for millions of minutes, thousands of hours, hundreds of days, scores of weeks, months, and for as many years as God gives you and for as many years as the work—or the dream!—requires.

God's Plan for Diligence

God is faithful to show us His plan and His path for a better life. There's no guesswork! And would you believe it? Diligence is a major theme throughout the Bible, especially in the book of Proverbs. There we learn that...

❧ Diligence affects our finances—"He who has a slack hand becomes poor, but the hand of the diligent makes rich" (Proverbs 10:4).

❧ Diligence affects our livelihood—"He who tills his land will be satisfied with bread, but he who follows frivolity is devoid of understanding" (Proverbs 12:11).

❧ Diligence affects our income and productivity—"In all labor there is profit, but idle chatter leads only to poverty" (Proverbs 14:23).

❧ Diligence affects our contribution to society—"He who is slothful in his work is a brother to him who is a great destroyer" (Proverbs 18:9).

❧ Diligence affects our outcome—"Be diligent to know the state of your flocks, and attend to your herds; for riches are not forever" (Proverbs 27:23-24).

❧ Diligence affects our comfort—"He who tills his land will have plenty of bread, but he who follows frivolity will have poverty enough" (Proverbs 28:19).

❧ Diligence affects our households (Proverbs 31:10-31).

We also learn that the diligent woman...

...rises while it is yet night (Proverbs 31:15),

...girds herself with strength (verse 17),

...strengthens her arms (verse 17),

...works into the night (verse 18), and

...does not eat the bread of idleness (verse 27).

Therefore…

>…her husband has no lack of gain (verse 11),
>
>…she provides food for her household (verse 15),
>
>…she makes tapestries for her home (verse 22), and
>
>…her clothing is fine linen and purple (verse 22).

And then the reward…

>…her children rise up and call her blessed (verse 28),
>
>…her husband also, and he praises her: "Many daughters have done well, but you excel them all" (verses 28-29),
>
>…she receives the fruit of her hands (verse 31), and
>
>…her own works praise her in the gates (verse 31).

Motivators for Diligence

If diligence accomplishes all of this (and more), and if diligence is this important for a better life, then what can help us become even more motivated in our perseverance? Consider these major contributors to diligence.

Awareness of the brevity of life—Many people choose to live life in a waiting mode, with an "I'll get around to it" attitude or an "I have all the time in the world" outlook. But the Bible teaches us the opposite, that life is brief (Psalm 39:4-5). In fact, God refers to our life as a vapor (James 4:14), as a breath (Job 7:7), and as a shadow (1 Chronicles 29:15).

Dear reading friend, there simply are no guarantees on the length of your life or my life! Our days are numbered... a number that only God knows. Therefore we must live each day to the hilt, to the max! We need to seize each and every day...and put the most into each 24 hours. We must do as much as we can, love our families as much as we can, help as many people as we can, give as much as we can in each precious sunrise-to-sunset parcel of life. Each part and parcel of each day, and each person in our every day—our marriages, our families, our homes, our ministries, our minutes, our work—must be relished and used wisely and fully...for it may be all we have.

Let your awareness of the brevity of life be a driving force. It will shine a new kind of light on the importance of discovering new daily steps for living God's plan. That's what the better-life person does. By contrast, fools squander, waste, and fritter away their time and their lives (Proverbs 18:9). Would you like to know how to waste a day? Just sleep in instead of getting up and getting going. Choose to sit or lie around instead of working (Proverbs 6:9).

Everyone is tempted with laziness (1 Corinthians 10:13), that's the nature of our flesh. It's a common problem. But the "I want a better life" woman doesn't rest when she should be working. Success and accomplishment is a simple formula: The person who works for eight hours will accomplish twice as much as the one who works only four. And the person who labors for twelve hours will produce twice as much as the one who only works six. It's just as the Bible says—"In all labor there is profit" (Proverbs 14:23), no matter what that labor is. (And the flip side of this verse is also true—"Idle chatter leads only to poverty.") So what will it be for you? The better use of life...or the waste of life?

Awareness of the purpose of life—Understanding the truth about God's plan and purpose for your life is another catalyst to diligence. When we realize that we were made *by* God and *for* God, and that God has a purpose for each of our lives, we don't live with "self" in mind. We instead begin living each day and each minute in each day for the Lord (Colossians 3:23). There's a new energy, a new direction, a new diligence, a serious soberness. And all of this because we suddenly grasp that God has a plan and a purpose for us.

Awareness of stewardship—With a sharp awareness of the brevity of life and the purpose of life, yet another contributor to diligence dawns on us. We begin to realize that each day and minute (and second!) of our lives is a gift from God. That means God intends us to manage our time and our lives *for Him* and to use them *for His purposes*. He intends that we live out His plan for us. That means God expects each of us to be a good steward of the life He entrusts us with. And what does the Bible say God requires of a steward? That he or she be faithful (1 Corinthians 4:2). One day every Christian will give an accounting to God for the use of his or her life (2 Corinthians 5:10). Seek to live each day with stewardship in mind for that one day. This mindset stimulates daily diligence.

Awareness of time—Or should I say, awareness of the time of day? I don't know about you, but I have peaks and valleys in my day. During my peak periods, I'm running on all cylinders. I'm moving at the speed of light! Things are happening! There's fire in my eyes and fervor in my steps.

But during my valley times, when my energy is at a lower level, why, I can hardly get up out of my chair! I don't seem to have an ounce of energy left. I seem to be done, finished, kaput(!)...and it's only 2:00 P.M.! Do these two scenarios sound familiar?

Well, I've learned (through persistence and training, which equals discipline!) that during down times you and I can still be productive and diligent by preparing for them (and believe me, they *will* come!) and by having a list of things we can do that take a lower level of energy. Things like preparing tomorrow's menus...folding that pile of freshly washed clothes...making phone calls...working a Bible correspondence course (I completed a whole series of Bible courses while my children were taking their naps).

So diligence doesn't mean maintaining a frantic pace of life from start to finish. No, diligence simply means pursuing a fruitful pace of life from start to finish as you purposefully move through the peaks and valleys, the ebb and flow, the springs, summers, and winters of your life.

An Example of Diligence

When I think of diligence, I can't help but think of Ruth in the Old Testament.

Meet Ruth

Ruth had a hard life. She had lost her husband. She had left her country. And then she had to provide for her mother-in-law. If Ruth hadn't been diligent, she and her mother-in-law, Naomi, might have starved to death. Talk about motivation! But the real insight on Ruth's character (because that's what diligence is—a mark of character) comes from what was said about her attitude toward her responsibilities by another:

> It has been fully reported to me, all that you have *done* for your mother-in-law since the death of your husband, and how you have left your father and your mother and the land of your birth, and have come to a people whom you did not know before. The Lord repay your *work* (Ruth 2:11-12).

My friend, our diligence should not be seen as a duty, but as a delight. Diligence comes from within and reveals our true character. Let's follow in the footsteps of Ruth's diligence and trust the results to the Lord. For as Ruth experienced, the Lord will repay our work and diligence.

Just for Today...

How can you become a woman of greater diligence? I'm sure by this time you know the answer...one day at a time. And how do you go about creating a better life for yourself and others? Through living God's plan, which includes faithful diligence practiced today...and extending into tomorrow...and continuing for a lifetime.

❏ Just for today...write out, memorize, and carry with you Colossians 3:23-24—"And whatever you do, do it heartily, as to the Lord and not to men, knowing that from the Lord you will receive the reward of the inheritance; for you serve the Lord Christ." Also ask yourself, "Since life is brief, how can I best spend this day?" Picture yourself as a steward. How will you answer to God for this day?

❏ Just for tomorrow...evaluate your peaks and valleys and plan in advance for them. Keep thinking of your tomorrow with an eye to stewardship. How are you planning for its use? Design your day...step-by-step, by the minute. Then follow that blueprint...just for the day. Read the corresponding chapter of Proverbs for that day. You'll probably find several verses dealing with diligence. Whatever you do, don't lose them! Take note of them for your life, make note of them in your journal, and carry out any small changes that will better your life!

❏ Just for this week...continue reading each day's chapter of Proverbs, noting and listing all the verses regarding this all-important area of diligence, work, industry, and perseverance. Continue planning for each day. At the end of your week, evaluate how you did and what corrections are needed next week. This is a process you'll want to repeat for the rest of your life. The result? By God's grace, a better life! It ought to be—it's a life lived by His guidance!

Living God's Plan

A key way to live out God's plan for your life—your better life—is to take to heart this word from Moses: "So teach us to number our days, that we may gain a heart of wisdom" (Psalm 90:12). Again, we don't know the number of our days, but Moses speculated that "the days of our lives are seventy years; and if by reason of strength they are eighty years" (verse 10). According to Moses, we just might live to be 70 or 80. So...let's do the math. How old are you today? Subtract that age from 70. What's the number? If God wills, that might be the number of years you have left to change and grow, to follow God's plan, and to live a better life. And believe me, it will be a life marked by diligence.

And now, my friend, we're at our journey's end. We must leave one another to go about the business of bettering our lives. But just think what can be accomplished for God and for others when you walk in godliness and diligence for your remaining years! Don't waste your most important resource—your life. Number your days. And use each and every one of them for God's glory and the good of others. That's definitely going to be a good life, a better life, and the best life. And, dear one, it will be a blessed life!

*G*od's *G*uidelines for a *B*etter *L*ife

⁓

- ❧ Get up...and get going...and keep going!—*"Go to the ant, you sluggard! Consider her ways and be wise. How long will you slumber, O sluggard? When will you rise from your sleep?"* (Proverbs 6:6,9).

- ❧ Give your all to every task, big or small—*"Whatever your hand finds to do, do it with your might"* (Ecclesiastes 9:10).

- ❧ As you do your work diligently, keep in mind for whom you are doing it—*"And whatever you do, do it heartily, as to the Lord and not to men, knowing that from the Lord you will receive the reward of the inheritance; for you serve the Lord Christ"* (Colossians 3:23-24).

- ❧ Don't let up or be discouraged because your reward is sure to come—*"And let us not grow weary while doing good, for in due season we shall reap if we do not lose heart"* (Galatians 6:9).

- ❧ Keep on keeping on, knowing your efforts for the Lord are never wasted—*"Be steadfast, immovable, always abounding in the work of the Lord, knowing that your labor is not in vain in the Lord"* (1 Corinthians 15:58).

Notes

Chapter 1—Ask for Wisdom

1. Michael Kendrick and Daryl Lucas, eds., *365 Life Lessons from Bible People* (Wheaton, IL: Tyndale House Publishers, 1996), p. 140.
2. Charles Haddon Spurgeon.
3. Charles R. Swindoll, *The Tale of the Tardy Oxcart*, quoting from his book *The Strong Family* (Nashville: Word Publishing, 1998), p. 613.
4. Ibid., quoting from his book *Living on the Ragged Edge*, p. 613.
5. M.R. De Haan and Henry G. Bosch, *Bread for Each Day* (Grand Rapids, MI: Zondervan Publishing House, 1980), April 16.

Chapter 2—Order Your Life

1. Charles R. Swindoll, *The Tale of the Tardy Oxcart*, quoting Wayne Martindale, *The Quotable Lewis* (Nashville: Word Publishing, 1998), p. 468.
2. Elizabeth George.
3. Swindoll, *Tale of the Tardy Oxcart*, p. 468.

Chapter 4—Read Your Bible

1. Albert M. Wells Jr., ed., *Inspiring Quotations—Contemporary & Classical* (Nashville: Thomas Nelson Publishers, 1988), p. 17.
2. Mark Porter, *The Time of Your Life* (Wheaton, IL: Victor Books, 1983), p. 114.

Chapter 5—Develop Your Prayer Life

1. Charles Bridges, *A Modern Study of the Book of Proverbs*, rev. by George F. Santa (Milford, MI: Mott Media, 1978), p. 17.
2. Author unknown, quoted in Eleanor L. Doan, *The Speaker's Sourcebook* (Grand Rapids, MI: Zondervan Publishing House, 1997), p. 196.

Chapter 6—Pursue Spiritual Growth

1. *Checklist for Life for Men*, quoting Jean-Nicolas Grou (Nashville: Thomas Nelson Publishers, 2002), p. 183.

2. Thomas à Kempis, *The Imitation of Christ—Book 1* (Macon, GA: Mercer University Press, 1989), pp. 11-12.

3. John 11:25.

4. 1 Peter 2:2 and 2 Peter 3:18.

5. Ephesians 2:5.

6. For your personal Bible study, please see Elizabeth George's ten Bible Studies for Busy Women. A listing is in the back of this book.

7. Mark Porter, *The Time of Your Life* (Wheaton, IL: Victor Books, 1983), p. 114.

8. George B. Chisholm, quoted in Sherwood Eliot Wirt and Kersten Beckstrom, *Topical Encyclopedia of Living Quotations* (Minneapolis: Bethany House Publishers, 1982), p. 152.

Chapter 7—Manage Your Life

1. Author unknown.

2. Edward R. Dayton and Ted W. Engstrom, *Strategy for Living* (Glendale, CA: G/L Publications, 1978), p. 175.

3. Proverbs 31:10-31; Ephesians 5:22-24,33; 1 Timothy 2:9-15; Titus 2:3-5.

4. Elizabeth George, *A Woman After God's Own Heart*® (Eugene, OR: Harvest House Publishers, 1997).

5. Dayton and Engstrom, *Strategy for Living*, p. 180.

Chapter 8—Live by a Schedule

1. W. Marshall Craig, quoted in Frank S. Mead, *12,000 Religious Quotations* (Grand Rapids, MI: Baker Book House, 1989), p. 269.

2. Roy B. Zuck, *The Speaker's Quote Book*, adapted from *Gospel-Lite* (Grand Rapids: Kregel Publications, 1997), p. 126.

Chapter 9—Care for Your Home

1. Author unknown, quoted in Eleanor L. Doan, *The Speaker's Sourcebook* (Grand Rapids: Zondervan Publishing House, 1977), p. 267.

2. Elizabeth George, *God's Wisdom for Little Girls* (Eugene, OR: Harvest House Publishers, 2000).

Chapter 10—Invest in Your Marriage

1. Marriage service from *The Book of Common Worship* (Philadelphia: Board of Christian Education of the Presbyterian Church, 1974).

2. These ten principles are drawn from Elizabeth George, *A Wife After God's Own Heart* (Eugene, OR: Harvest House Publishers, 2004).

3. For more information on child-raising, read Elizabeth George, *A Mom After God's Own Heart* (Eugene, OR: Harvest House Publishers, 2005).

Chapter 11—Train Your Children

1. Derek Kidner, *The Proverbs* (Downers Grove, IL: InterVarsity Press, 1973), p. 147.
2. William MacDonald, *Enjoying the Proverbs* (Kansas City, KS: Walterick Publishers, 1982), p. 55.
3. Albert M. Wells Jr., ed., *Inspiring Quotations—Contemporary & Classical* (Nashville: Thomas Nelson Publishers, 1988), p. 106.

Chapter 12—Love Your Children

1. Elisabeth Elliot, *The Shaping of a Christian Family*, quoting an anonymous source (Nashville: Thomas Nelson Publishers, 1991), pp. 95-96.
2. Derek Kidner, *The Proverbs* (Downers Grove, IL: InterVarsity Press, 1973), p. 183.
3. Ibid. Proverbs 31:2 is an example of staircase parallelism, where each phrase repeats something from the prior phrase yet adds something new.
4. Michael Kendrick and Daryl Lucas, eds., *365 Life Lessons from Bible People* (Wheaton, IL: Tyndale House Publishers, 1996), p. 355.

Chapter 13—Cultivate Inner Beauty

1. Charles Bridges, *A Modern Study of the Book of Proverbs*, rev. by George F. Santa (Milford, MI: Mott Media, 1978), p. 738.
2. Neil S. Wilson, ed., *The Handbook of Bible Application* (Wheaton, IL: Tyndale House Publishers, 1992), pp. 56-57.
3. D.L. Moody, *Notes from My Bible and Thoughts from My Library* (Grand Rapids: Baker Book House, 1979), p. 19.
4. See Elizabeth George, *A Woman After God's Own Heart®*, *A Young Woman After God's Own Heart*, and *A Woman After God's Own Heart® Bible Study Series* (Eugene, OR: Harvest House Publishers).

Chapter 14—Tend to Your Appearance

1. John MacArthur, *The MacArthur Study Bible* (Nashville: Word Publishing, 1997), p. 1863.
2. Charles Caldwell Ryrie, *The Ryrie Study Bible* (Chicago: Moody Press, 1978), p. 1817.
3. Ibid.
4. Ibid.
5. William MacDonald, *Enjoying the Proverbs* (Kansas City, KS: Walterick Publishers, 1982), p. 44.
6. John MacArthur Jr., *The MacArthur New Testament Commentary—1 Timothy* (Chicago: Moody Press, 1995), pp. 80-81.

7. Denis Waitley, quoted in Elizabeth George, *Life Management for Busy Women* (Eugene, OR: Harvest House Publishers, 2002), p. 80.

Chapter 15—Watch What You Eat

1. Elisabeth Elliot, *Discipline, the Glad Surrender* (Grand Rapids, MI: Fleming H. Revell, 1982), pp. 46-47.
2. William MacDonald, *Enjoying the Proverbs* (Kansas City, KS: Walterick Publishers, 1982), p. 126.
3. Derek Kidner, *The Proverbs* (Downers Grove, IL: InterVarsity Press, 1973), p. 152.
4. Ralph Wardlaw, *Lectures on the Book of Proverbs, Volume III* (Minneapolis: Klock & Klock Christian Publishers, 1982), p. 91.
5. Ibid., p. 99.
6. Charles R. Swindoll, *The Tale of the Tardy Oxcart*, quoting from *The Strong Family* (Nashville: Word Publishing, 1998), p. 613.
7. "Restrain yourself! Don't stuff yourself." These are the literal translations of the words "put a knife to your throat" according to Robert L. Alden, *Proverbs, A Commentary on an Ancient Book of Timeless Advice* (Grand Rapids, MI: Baker Book House, 1990), p. 168.

Chapter 16—Eat Just Enough

1. D.L. Moody, *Notes from My Bible and Thoughts from My Library* (Grand Rapids, MI: Baker Book House, 1979), p. 269.
2. Curtis Vaughan, *The Old Testament Books of Poetry from 26 Translations* (Grand Rapids, MI: Zondervan Bible Publishers, 1973), pp. 622-23.
3. Robert L. Alden, *Proverbs, A Commentary on an Ancient Book of Timeless Advice* (Grand Rapids, MI: Baker Book House, 1990), p. 208.
4. Robert Jamieson, A.R. Fausset, and David Brown, *Commentary on the Whole Bible* (Grand Rapids, MI: Zondervan Publishing House, 1973), p. 1199.
5. John MacArthur, *The MacArthur Study Bible* (Nashville: Word Publishing, 1997), p. 737.
6. William MacDonald, *Enjoying the Proverbs* (Kansas City, KS: Walterick Publishers, 1982), p. 126.

Chapter 17—Grow in Discipline

1. Thomas à Kempis, *The Imitation of Christ—Book 1* (Macon, GA: Mercer University Press, 1989), p. 32.
2. Ibid.
3. Harry Emerson Fosdick, 1878–1969.

Bibliography

Alden, Robert L. *Proverbs, a Commentary on an Ancient Book of Timeless Advice*. Grand Rapids, MI: Baker Book House, 1990.

Kidner, Derek. *The Proverbs*. Downers Grove, IL: InterVarsity Press, 1973.

MacDonald, William. *Enjoying the Proverbs*. Kansas City, KS: Walterick Publishers, 1982. Walterick Publishers, P.O. Box 2216, Kansas City, KS 66110.

Santa, George F. *A Modern Study in the Book of Proverbs,* Charles Bridges' Classic Revised for Today's Reader. Milford, MI: Mott Media, 1978.

Wardlaw, Ralph. *Lectures on the Book of Proverbs, Volumes 1-3*. Minneapolis: Klock & Klock Christian Publishers, 1982.

Wiersbe, Warren W. *Be Skillful*. Colorado Springs: Chariot Victor Publishing, a division of Cook Communications, 1995.

Personal Notes

_____

_____

_____

_____

_____

_____

_____

_____

_____

_____

_____

_____

_____

_____

_____

_____

_____

Personal Notes

Personal Notes

Personal Notes

Personal Notes

_____

_____

_____

_____

_____

_____

_____

_____

_____

_____

_____

_____

_____

_____

_____

_____

_____

Personal Notes

_____

_____

_____

_____

_____

_____

_____

_____

_____

_____

_____

_____

_____

_____

_____

_____

_____

_____

Personal Notes

_____

_____

_____

_____

_____

_____

_____

_____

_____

_____

_____

_____

_____

_____

_____

_____

_____

_____

If you've benefited from *Small Changes for a Better Life,* you'll want the companion volume

Small Changes *for a* Better Life

GROWTH
AND
STUDY GUIDE

Live out God's plan and enjoy the success that comes! This exciting guide will help you. It provides additional questions, scriptures, exercises, and life-changing applications that will put you on the fast track to a better life. This growth and study guide is perfect for both personal and group use.

Small Changes for a Better Life
Growth and Study Guide is available at your local Christian bookstore or can be ordered from:

Jim and Elizabeth George Ministries
PO Box 2879
Belfair, WA 98528
Toll-free fax/phone: 1-800-542-4611
or at
www.ElizabethGeorge.com
www.JimGeorge.com

About the Author

Elizabeth George is a bestselling author who has more than 3.4 million books in print. She's a popular speaker at Christian women's events. Her passion is to teach the Bible in a way that changes women's lives. For information about Elizabeth's books or speaking ministry, to sign up for her mailings, or to share how God has used this book in your life, please write to Elizabeth at:

Elizabeth George
P.O. Box 2879
Belfair, WA 98528

Toll-free fax/phone:
1-800-542-4611
www.ElizabethGeorge.com

A Woman After God's Own Heart® Study Series

Bible Studies for Busy Women

"God wrote the Bible to change hearts and lives. Every study in this series is written with that in mind—and is especially focused on helping Christian women know how God desires for them to live."

—Elizabeth George

Sharing wisdom gleaned from more than 20 years as a women's Bible study teacher, Elizabeth has prepared insightful lessons that can be completed in 15 to 20 minutes per day. Each lesson includes thought-provoking questions, insights, Bible-study tips, instructions for leading a discussion group, and a "heart response" section to make the Bible passage more personal.

Living with Passion and Purpose — LUKE — Elizabeth George
978-0-7369-0816-0

Becoming a Woman of Beauty & Strength — ESTHER — Elizabeth George
978-0-7369-0489-6

Putting On a Gentle & Quiet Spirit — 1 PETER — Elizabeth George
978-0-7369-0290-8

Discovering the Treasures of a Godly Woman — PROVERBS 31 — Elizabeth George
978-0-7369-0818-4

Nurturing a Heart of Humility — CHARACTER STUDIES/MARY — Elizabeth George
978-0-7369-0300-4

Walking in God's Promises — CHARACTER STUDIES/SARAH — Elizabeth George
978-0-7369-0301-1

Experiencing God's Peace — PHILIPPIANS — Elizabeth George
978-0-7369-0289-2

Pursuing Godliness — 1 TIMOTHY — Elizabeth George
978-0-7369-0665-4

Cultivating a Life of Character — JUDGES/RUTH — Elizabeth George
978-0-7369-0498-8

Growing in Wisdom & Faith — JAMES — Elizabeth George
978-0-7369-0490-2

HARVEST HOUSE PUBLISHERS
EUGENE, OREGON 97402
www.harvesthousepublishers.com

Powerful Promises for Every Woman

by Elizabeth George

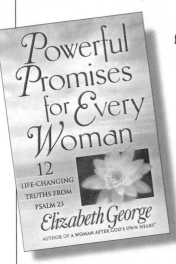

Do you desire greater strength for today and help for all your tomorrows? Discover 12 life-changing promises from God's Word that can carry you through every day and every season of life...promises that truly refresh and encourage, bringing purpose and hope in the midst of life's frantic pace. Even in your seemingly impossible situations, you can know that God's resources are available to you through His promises!

Join Elizabeth George on a powerful journey through Psalm 23 and become a woman whose daily life is energized by God's enabling promises.

For deeper personal or group study—
Powerful Promises for Every Woman
Growth and Study Guide.

A Mom After God's Own Heart

by Elizabeth George

*Catch God's heart
for Your Children*

You want to raise children who are happy and successful, and who follow after God. But how do you do that in this day of hectic schedules? With biblical wisdom and plenty of encouragement, Elizabeth George offers time-proven ideas and valuable suggestions to help you nurture children of all ages in the Lord. You'll discover...

* Easy-to-implement principles that make parenting enjoyable and effective
* Specific ways you can teach your children that God loves and cares for them
* "Little Choices" you can put into practice immediately to make a big impact
* Special parenting insights and strategies from a Christian dad

Help your children experience God's love, God's blessings, and God's provisions.

For more in-depth and personal or group study—
A Mom After God's Own Heart Growth and Study Guide.

Books by Elizabeth George

- Beautiful in God's Eyes
- Life Management for Busy Women
- Loving God with All Your Mind
- A Mom After God's Own Heart
- Powerful Promises for Every Woman
- The Remarkable Women of the Bible
- Small Changes for a Better Life
- A Wife After God's Own Heart
- A Woman After God's Own Heart®
- A Woman After God's Own Heart® Deluxe Edition
- A Woman's Call to Prayer
- A Woman's High Calling
- A Woman's Walk with God
- A Young Woman After God's Own Heart
- A Young Woman's Call to Prayer
- A Young Woman's Walk with God

Children's Books

- God's Wisdom for Little Girls

Study Guides

- Beautiful in God's Eyes Growth & Study Guide
- Life Management for Busy Women Growth & Study Guide
- Loving God with All Your Mind Growth & Study Guide
- A Mom After God's Own Heart Growth & Study Guide
- Powerful Promises for Every Woman Growth & Study Guide
- The Remarkable Women of the Bible Growth & Study Guide
- Small Changes for a Better Life Growth & Study Guide
- A Wife After God's Own Heart Growth & Study Guide
- A Woman After God's Own Heart® Growth & Study Guide
- A Woman's Call to Prayer Growth & Study Guide
- A Woman's High Calling Growth & Study Guide
- A Woman's Walk with God Growth & Study Guide

Books by Jim & Elizabeth George

- God Loves His Precious Children
- God's Wisdom for Little Boys

Books by Jim George

- God's Man of Influence
- A Husband After God's Own Heart
- A Man After God's Own Heart
- The Remarkable Prayers of the Bible
- The Remarkable Prayers of the Bible Growth & Study Guide
- A Young Man After God's Own Heart